KT-226-071

# The Last Woman to be Hanged

## *The Ruth Ellis Story*

### Robert Hancock

SEVEN DIALS

First published as *Ruth Ellis* in Great Britain in 1963 by
George Weidenfeld & Nicolson Ltd
This paperback edition published in 2020 by Seven Dials
an imprint of The Orion Publishing Group Ltd
Carmelite House, 50 Victoria Embankment
London EC4Y 0DZ

An Hachette UK Company

1 3 5 7 9 10 8 6 4 2

Copyright © Robert Hancock 1963, 2000

Documents provided by the Public Record Office
references: HO291/237, PCOM9/2084, HO291/235,
HO291/238 © Crown Copyright
Internal images © Mirrorpix

The moral right of Robert Hancock to be identified as
the author of this work has been asserted in accordance with
the Copyright, Designs and Patents Act of 1988.

All rights reserved. No part of this publication may be
reproduced, stored in a retrieval system, or transmitted
in any form or by any means, electronic, mechanical,
photocopying, recording, or otherwise, without the prior
permission of both the copyright owner and the above
publisher of this book.

A CIP catalogue record for this book is
available from the British Library.

ISBN (Mass Market Paperback) 978 1 8418 8447 9
ISBN (eBook) 978 1 8418 8448 6

Printed and bound in Great Britain by Clays Ltd, Elcograf S.p.A.

www.orionbooks.co.uk

In his classic biography of Ruth Ellis, the last woman hanged in Britain, Robert Hancock tells a true story which reads almost like fiction.

Since childhood, Ruth Ellis learnt quickly what she wanted from life: to escape from poverty-stricken post-war Brixton and all that it stood for. As a model, hostess and finally manageress of the 'Little Club' in West End London, she became involved in a series of stormy, alcohol-driven relationships. Her obsession with one of her most violent lovers ended in her killing him. In court she showed no remorse, remaining virtually impassive – but was this reason enough to condemn her to death?

Windsor and Maidenhead

95800000165670

Robert Hancock, the pseudonym of Douglas Howell, was born in Surrey in 1920 and educated at Monmouth School and Queen's College, Oxford. During the Second World War he was a lieutenant in the Royal Artillery and was taken prisoner at Tobruk. He was a POW in Italy and then Germany until the end of the war.

After the war he entered journalism and became a reporter for the *Daily Mirror* until 1953, when he joined the *Sunday Express*. In 1955 he left the Beaverbrook Group to become a features writer on *Woman's Sunday Mirror* and a regular contributor to *The Spectator*. In 1957 he joined the *Sunday Pictorial* (later the *Sunday Mirror)* as a features writer. In 1969 he worked on secondment for nine months as Special Assistant to the Postmaster General, John Stonehouse MP. He returned briefly to the *Sunday Mirror* but was then offered the job as Group Public Relations Adviser at Lew Grade's ATV. When ATV became Central Television he was Head of their London Press Office until he retired in 1985.

Robert Hancock was married, with four sons, and lived in London. He died in 2007.

# Contents

*For Richard, John,*
*William and Robert*

# Foreword

My interest in Mrs Ruth Ellis began in the spring of 1955 when the now vanished newspaper *Woman's Sunday Mirror* bought her life story and I wrote it for them. Like all newspaper stories of this kind it was an occasionally obscure and sometimes misleading account; unlike some newspaper life stories it also contained enough truth to make it interesting.

The reason why the Ruth Ellis story was not fully told was threefold. The first and most important reason was the character of the editor, the late James Eilbeck, then aged thirty.

Jim Eilbeck with his bushy RAF model ginger moustache (flat feet had barred him from the Forces) began his newspaper career in his home town, Liverpool. He always retained a provincial's illusion that London night clubs are exciting places filled with glamour, wealth and the famous. When he heard that Ruth Ellis, a model who had once been a night club hostess, had shot her lover, a racing car driver, he immediately projected the story as one of champagne, high life and excitement. He was chagrined, but not deterred, when he discovered that Ruth Ellis was a call girl who had unsuccessfully taken a modelling course, and that David Blakely, the man she murdered, was a weak, impoverished and in many ways most ungallant character.

Jim Eilbeck could not have printed all the truth even if he had been willing; Ruth Ellis and the legal halters that restrain, often unfairly, British journalism, would have stopped that.

Ruth Ellis herself was determined not to authorize a story that revealed the sad, mad nature of her character or, for example, that for years she had made money from prostitution and posing for pornographic pictures.

Ruth Ellis was a woman of obsessive pride and when she became manageress of the 'Little Club', that second-rate upstairs drinking room in Knightsbridge, she felt that she was at last someone of importance. Like most self-made successes she did not want too much told of the sluttish and often disgraceful byways she had travelled before she reached the Harrods belt, Mecca of the pushers and comfort of that section of the middle class predestined for disappearance or absorption. It was in this area that the affair between Ruth, the pusher from the grey stifle of Brixton, and David Blakely, the lazy son of middle-class comfort, lived and lusted.

The third reason why all the facts, or as many as were available at the time, never appeared in the *Woman's Sunday Mirror* was that when the series appeared Mrs Ellis was awaiting execution. Although she had not appealed against her sentence, both she and her legal advisers believed that she would be reprieved. Consequently anything that her lawyers felt could prejudice a reprieve was removed from the story.

The night before her execution she wrote to a friend: 'I must close now but remember I am quite happy with the verdict, but not the way the story was told, there is so much that people don't know about.'

There will always be much that nobody will ever discover about Ruth Ellis and David Blakely, for both these important witnesses are dead, but this book, within the limits of the human memory of those who have been prepared to help, is as much of the truth as I can discover. Many passages are based on the long and frank conversations I had with that sad, shocked man, Desmond Cussen, in the weeks that preceded Ruth Ellis's trial at the Old Bailey and during the time she waited for her execution on 13 July, 1955, at Holloway Prison.

Desmond Cussen was described at the Old Bailey trial as 'her alternative lover'. At one time in her affair with David Blakely she had been living with Desmond Cussen, but she also spent as many nights as possible with Blakely at a Kensington hotel.

You can dismiss the story as one of useless, worthless people; if you do then you are either a hypocrite or a fool.

The everyday world of men and women is not the deodorized, glossy lies of the TV commercial and the woman's magazine. There is a David Blakely in every man and a Ruth Ellis in every woman.

# I

# Death on Easter Sunday

The grey-green Vanguard van whose commercial metal side panels had been replaced by windows, stopped exactly outside the saloon bar entrance to the public house. The driver and passenger, both men, got out, the passenger locking his door with the catch and the driver his with a key.

They walked across the wide pavement into the saloon bar of the 'Magdala', an unpretentious Charrington's house at the bottom of South Hill Park, in the North London suburb of Hampstead. It was a hilly road, composed of dejected late Victorian houses and sprinkled with useful, small shops.

A few of the Sunday night regulars at the pub greeted the men as they went to the bar but they got no particular attention. The owner and driver of the Vanguard was David Blakely, twenty-five years old and by occupation the works manager of a small engineering firm at Penn in Buckinghamshire. Whenever possible this dark, weakly handsome man would drive racing cars at home and abroad.

A sticker on the rear window of his van announced the forthcoming *Daily Express* trophy meeting at Silverstone on 7 May 1955. His companion was Clive Gunnell, thirty, a fair-haired man of slightly blurred good looks, by trade a Mayfair car salesman; he lived nearby at No. 45 South Hill Park.

The landlord, Mr Colson, knew Blakely well enough to accept his cheques and the first thing at the bar Blakely did that Easter Sunday evening was to cash a cheque for five pounds. It was about nine o'clock. After a few drinks, beer for Gunnell, gin and tonic for Blakely, Blakely bought three quarts of light ale and some cigarettes to take them back to a party they had temporarily left. Neither of them noticed a slight, blonde woman, wearing heavy black-rimmed spectacles, peering through the bar window, her head wreathed by the sign in the glass WINES. One of the customers saw her but took no particular notice; there is nothing unusual about a shy woman looking through the window of a pub to see if the man she is meeting has arrived.

The two friends drank up and went out into the dimly lit street. Gunnell, who left the pub a few steps before Blakely, walked round the car to the passenger door and waited for his friend to get in to release the catch. Blakely, who was carrying one of the flagons of beer, fumbled for his car keys in the pockets of his grey suit.

The platinum blonde walking down the hill towards the car called out 'David'. He ignored her. She opened her bag, took out a heavy, black revolver and pointed it at him.

In moments of danger a man normally has two reactions: to fight or run. David Blakely started to run towards the back of the car and the landlord inside the 'Magdala' heard the first two shots. He, like Clive Gunnell, who was still waiting on the other side of the van, thought that the bangs were fireworks fixed by Blakely to explode as a warning if anyone tried to steal the car.

As Blakely reached the back of the car he screamed 'Clive' and ran towards him. Some of the blood from his wounds stippled the two rear grey doors of the van. Blood spotted the chromium bumper and smudged the dark green paint of the two-tone colour scheme.

Still carrying the gun the blonde chased the wounded man round the car; Gunnell was motionless. 'Get out of the way, Clive,' she shouted. Blakely had reached the bonnet, rounded it, and was again running uphill. The blonde fired again. By now Gunnell had recovered from the paralysis of the unexpected and followed the pair round the bonnet of the Vanguard. He saw the woman standing over Blakely, who was lying face down on the pavement. His head pointed uphill, just level with the row of newspaper bill-boards outside the shop next door to the pub.

The blonde was firing at Blakely's back but her control of the gun was poor and one shot hit a passerby in the thumb. She was the wife of a bank official and had the poetic name of Mrs Gladys Kensington Yule. Mrs Yule was on her way for a drink at the 'Magdala' with her husband.

It was probably the last shot from the six-chambered •38 Smith and Wesson that wounded Mrs Yule. The irreparable damage had been done to Blakely and the blood was rivu-leting from his mouth on to the pavement. Here it mixed with the frothing remains of the beer flagon to which Blakely had somehow clung during the chase. Unmoved by the channel of red froth that moved past her down the hill, and the moaning of the man on the pavement, the blonde repeatedly clicked the now empty gun. In her left hand she held a black handbag by the strap. There was no blood on her grey two-piece suit nor on the green roll-topped pullo-ver she was wearing. The man was quiet now. A spectator loosened the Old Salopian tie from the throat of the unmov-ing body on the pavement.

A man by Hanshaw's, the newsagent and tobacconist,

outside which Blakely was lying on his stomach with his left cheek on the pavement, heard several clicks from the useless weapon. Someone in the small crowd collected by the centripetal force of disaster shouted to the woman: 'What have you done, you'll both die now!' Her face was white but composed. She stood with her back to the pub wall, waiting. As Gunnell lifted Blakely's head from the pavement she said: 'Now go and call the police.'

Obediently Gunnell ran into the pub and shouted to the landlord: 'She's got him.' Mr Colson telephoned for the police and an ambulance.

A customer from the saloon bar pushed his way to the woman; it was the man who had noticed her face at the bar window earlier. Without emotion and without turning her head she said to him: 'Phone the police.' It was one of those moments when life outstrips the efforts of the best dramatists.

With disciplined dignity he replied: 'I am a police officer.' He was Police Constable Alan Thompson, PC 389 of 'L' Division, Metropolitan Police, who was having an off-duty drink in plain clothes.

PC Thompson did not let dignity blind him to danger and he smartly removed the gun from the right hand of the unresisting blonde.

There were no tears and no hysterics from the woman; everyone just stood waiting for the ambulance and the police car. They arrived about four minutes later and ambulance men loaded Blakely inside. He was dead when the hospital doctor examined him. (The other casualty, Mrs Yule, had already been taken to hospital by a reluctant taxi driver who 'didn't want no trouble'.)

After the ambulance had gone, the woman, who was still

silent, was taken to Hampstead police station in a police car. Here they offered her the inevitable cup of tea and a cigarette. In exchange she identified herself. The time was about 11 pm, Sunday, 2 April, 1955.

'My name is Mrs Ruth Ellis. I am a model. I am twenty-eight and I live at 44 Egerton Gardens, that's Kensington.'

She was unbelievably calm and detached.

That is how witnesses outside and inside the 'Magdala', and the police, saw and later retold the story. Over a month after her arrest Ruth Ellis wrote this account of her reactions immediately before and after she shot David Blakely. By this time she had heard what the main prosecution witnesses had said at the preliminary hearings at Hampstead Magistrates Court; the euphoria of the killing had gone, she knew her life was desperately compromised. By now most women would have changed their attitude, and calmness would have become frantic, anxious, neck-saving remorse. Before the world, and probably in their hearts, they would have excused and regretted their actions.

In what she wrote there is the faintest dusting of excuse; there is no regret and no search for mercy. Through it all weaves the amazing composure that the police remarked upon at Hampstead:

'I felt somehow outside of myself – although I seemed to be registering impressions quite clearly – it did not seem to be me. I was in a sort of daze.

'When I got to Tanza Road I saw David's car drive away and I followed on foot down Tanza Road towards the "Magdala" where I saw the car outside. It must have been between 9 and 9.30 pm and I went down to the "Magdala" and stood for a few minutes a little way up the hill from the back of the car on the pavement. I certainly do not remember looking in the window of the "Magdala" and I do not think I did, although I walked down past the "Magdala" and up again. Anyway, after what seemed to me to be only a few minutes, I saw Clive Gunnell, followed by David, come out of the door of the "Magdala".

'I thought they were both carrying bottles. Clive went around to the nearside door – the car was facing downhill on the same side of the road as the "Magdala" and immediately outside the door [she means the bar door here] – David walked up to the door on the driving side – I have a vague impression that he saw me but went to the door of the car without taking any notice of me.

'I know I was in a frightful temper and I think I started forward and took the pistol out of my handbag as I was walking towards him. I believe I stopped a few paces away from him and fired but what he was doing or whether he was facing me or had his back to me – I cannot say – I just do not know.

'I did not hear him call out but he started running round the back of the Vanguard. I had no experience in firing a gun before and I did not think he had been hit because he was running.

'I think I followed and when I was beside Clive I said: "Stand still, Clive" or something like that – he was petrified and then when I got to the front of the bonnet of the car I think I fired again – David was still running and I must have followed because when I got back to the other side of the Vanguard on the pavement near the rear he was running along the pavement up the hill towards Tanza Road – he looked round as I shot again and he fell forward flat on his face.

'During the whole of this time I felt that I was in a kind

of cold frenzy but I am certain in my own mind that I did not fire at him when he was on the ground. At one time I seem to remember someone saying "Stop it, Ruth" – it may have been David – it may have been Clive, but I cannot see how it could have been David. In fact, I do not remember firing any more shots although the pistol must have been empty because I vaguely remember it clicking. I am sure there were no more shots because I meant to shoot myself.

'I remember standing there watching him in a completely detached sort of way – I did not feel anything except I seemed to be fascinated by the blood – I have never seen so much blood. He seemed to gasp two or three times, heaved and then relaxed. I think that must have been when he died. I saw his outstretched arm – his watch and signet ring. I was rooted to the spot – I neither moved nor spoke. I seemed to be looking at things in a sort of haze rather as if I were drunk – I remember Clive coming round to where David lay but I am sure I never said to him "Now, go and call the police" or anything like that. Someone felt David's pulse and said "He's gone." Clive was hysterical and screaming "Why did you kill him? Why didn't you kill me? What good is he to you dead? You'll both die now." Someone said "Pull yourself together, you're a man, aren't you?"

'Whilst all this was going on a man in civilian clothes came up to me. I said "Will you phone the police." He said "I am a policeman." I was still holding the gun and I said "Arrest me – I have just shot this man – and fetch an ambulance." He said "Stand there" and offered me a cigarette. I said "No, thank you."

'I stood beside David watching him until the ambulance arrived – it seemed a very long time. Someone eventually put a blanket over him. When the ambulance arrived they were slow putting him in. They asked lots of silly questions like "What's happened?" They put him in face down as he was. Clive said to the ambulance man – "I will go with you" and he went in the ambulance.

'Later on the police car arrived and I walked over to it. I heard someone say "Who did it?" and someone answered "She did." It all seemed rather far away but I had a curious feeling of relief. I got in the car and waited until a police-woman arrived. We drove to Hampstead police station where they took my property including my signet ring which had been bent all shapes – due to the fights I had had with David. Then they put me into a cell and I seemed to be waiting a long time. They came back with two CID men, one of them said "We have seen the dead body of David Moffett Drummond Blakely in the mortuary and are charging you with his murder." I said: "I am guilty. I am rather confused."

'Then they said something about not having to make a statement and they added "There must be quite a story at the back of all this – would you care to tell us about it?" At this time all I could see was a lot of blood and I was talking more or less mechanically as though I were in a dream. I know they asked me all sorts of questions like "When did you decide to do this? Did you plan to kill him tonight? Did you intend to kill him when you put the gun in your bag? Where did you get the gun from?" A man with glasses was asking all the questions.'

When she wrote this account Ruth Ellis endowed her actions with retrospective confusion and dream quality that she certainly did not show when arrested. Three hours after she arrived at the police station she made a statement before three CID officers, Detective Superintendent Leonard Crawford, Detective Chief Inspector Leslie Davies and

Detective Inspector Peter Gill. Inspector Davies was the CID man 'wearing glasses' and he was to be in charge of the case.

Admittedly, like most statements, it was not the spontaneous flow of recollected events that the law requires, but the result of question and answer by the suspect to the police. Often the police put words into the mouths of suspects but there was no suggestion that they did this with Ruth Ellis. Really confused people may mislead the police in their confusion; they seldom tell sustained deliberate lies.

What Ruth Ellis did within the time after the shooting was to concoct stories about the origin of the gun and the events immediately preceding the shooting that were boldly conceived and sustained lies.

Inspector Davies himself was never deceived about her 'confusion'. At the Old Bailey he was examined by Mr Christmas Humphreys for the Crown.

Q. What did Mr Crawford say to her?
A. Mr Crawford said to her: 'I have just seen the dead body of David Blakely at Hampstead Mortuary. I understand you know something about it' and he cautioned her.
Q. Just tell the jury what that means.
A. He said to her: 'You are not obliged to say anything at all about this unless you wish to do so, but whatever you say will be taken down in writing and may be given in evidence.'
Q. What did she say?
A. She said: 'I am guilty. I am rather confused,' and then she . . .
Q. Just a moment. Did you form any impression of her emotional condition at that time?

A. I did, my Lord. I was most impressed by the fact that she seemed very composed.

Q. I did ask you about her emotional condition. What about her mental condition when she said she was confused?

A. There was no sign of confusion in her manner, or attitude, my Lord, at all.

Inspector Davies then produced Ruth's statement.

'I understand what has been said. I am guilty. I am rather confused.

'About two years ago I met David Blakely when I was manageress of the Little Club, Knightsbridge; my flat was above that. I had known him for about a fortnight when he started to live with me and has done so continuously until last year when he went away to Le Mans for about three weeks motor racing. He came back to me and remained living with me until Good Friday morning.

'He left me about 10 am and promised to be back by 8 pm to take me out. I waited until half-past nine and he had not phoned, although he always had done in the past.

'I was rather worried at that stage as he had had trouble with his racing car and had been drinking.

'I rang some friends of his named Findlater at Hampstead but they told me he was not there, although David had told me he was visiting them. I was speaking to Mr Findlater and I asked if David was all right. He laughed and said: "Oh yes, he's all right." I did not believe he was not there and I took a taxi to Hampstead where I saw David's car outside Findlater's flat at 28 Tanza Road. I then telephoned from nearby and when my voice was recognized they hung up on me. I went to the flat and continually rang the door bell but they would not answer. I became very furious and went to

David's car which was still standing there and pushed in three of the side windows. The noise I made must have aroused the Findlaters as the police came along and spoke to me. Mr Findlater came out of his flat and the police also spoke to him.

'David did not come home on Saturday and at nine o'clock this morning [Sunday] I phoned the Findlaters again and Mr Findlater answered. I said to him: "I hope you are having an enjoyable holiday" and was about to say "Because you have ruined mine" and he banged the receiver down.

'I waited all day today [Sunday] for David to phone but he did not do so. About eight o'clock this evening [Sunday] I put my son Andria to bed.

'I then took a gun which I had hidden and put it in my handbag. This gun was given to me about three years ago in a club by a man whose name I do not remember. It was security for money but I accepted it as a curiosity. I did not know it was loaded when it was given to me but I knew next morning when I looked at it. When I put the gun in my bag I intended to find David and shoot him.

'I took a taxi to Tanza Road and as I arrived David's car drove away from Findlater's address. I dismissed the taxi and walked back down the road to the nearest pub where I saw David's car outside. I waited outside until he came out with a friend I know as Clive.'

The rest of the statement is a shortened version of Ruth's own account of the shooting that has already been given.

The only sign of confusion in this statement was that Ruth had mistaken the number of the house where the Findlaters lived; she said No. 28 instead of No. 29. This, in fact, may have been a clerical error by Inspector Peter Gill who wrote down the statement. Even allowing for the impersonality of the question and answer method by which it was compiled, ther is no emotion in the document. Ruth describes the shooting of the man with whom she has been living, like a male motorist reporting the running down of a stray dog. There is no indication of any real motive for the shooting and no reference to the fights, jealousies, reconciliations and midnight car chases that gave film-like quality to their relationship.

In times of upset and disaster a mother's immediate thoughts go to her children. It was only while her statement was being taken down that this woman casually disclosed that she had a son. Inspector Davies at first thought that this indifference meant that she had killed him before she left home.

He ordered a police car to check at the address, No. 44 Egerton Gardens, near South Kensington Underground Station, that Ruth Ellis had given him. Just before dawn a very relieved policewoman found ten-year-old Andria asleep on a camp bed in the rented furnished bed-sitting room that his mother had left the previous night when she set off to murder David Blakely.

It was to be the most discussed and controversial murder trial and verdict since the war and the execution of Ruth Ellis gave tremendous support to the abolitionist cause.

Ruth Ellis was the last woman to be hanged in Britain and her case was a powerful lever in establishing the law of 'diminished responsibility' incorporated in the Homicide Act of 1957. Today a woman who had been subjected to the same emotional pummelling that Ruth endured in the months before she murdered David would probably succeed with this plea. The execution of Ruth Ellis helped to speed the day when the hangman joined the headsman in the records of senseless historical curiosities.

# 2

# Ruth Ellis

Ruth Neilson (the Ellis was to be acquired by marriage later) was born on 9 October 1926, at No. 74 West Parade, a villa in the Welsh seaside town of Rhyl. Those who like to correlate the vagaries of the weather with historic events may care to know that it is reported that on that day there was a violent sandstorm on the beach. Her parents were ordinary, respectable and lower middle class. Her father, Arthur Neilson, was a musician from Manchester who played the 'cello on Atlantic liners; he had brought his family to Rhyl because it was handy for the port of Liverpool. Ruth's mother, Bertha, a refugee from Belgium, came to England during the first World War. No deep smouldering fire of Welsh passion and depression can be blamed for what was to happen, but those who believe that continental blood and *crimes passionnels* are synonymous will note that Ruth Neilson was half Belgian.

How much Ruth's later actions were conditioned by her childhood and early adolescence depends entirely on what you believe about the effects of environment and heredity. For those who believe, in the best pragmatic British tradition, that the truth is a nicely balanced fifty-fifty mixture, it is possible to see in Ruth Ellis's early life the formation of the central themes of her adult character.

For the first seven years of Ruth's life her mother, a

woman of incisive and logical personality, was the dominant influence, as her father was either away at sea, or playing in cinema and theatre orchestras around the country. The talkies were the beginning of the end for him, as for thousands of other musicians in the thirties.

In 1933 Arthur Neilson decided that unfortunately the talkies were here to stay and that he must find a secure job with which to keep his family of three girls and two boys. Like many a Northerner during prewar and postwar depressions, he moved South. He found a job at Basingstoke in Hampshire as a telephonist and hall porter at the Park Prewett Mental Hospital; a house went with the job.

Ruth attended the local elementary school, Fairfields Senior Girls' School. At thirteen she was a skinny, short-sighted girl with straight blonde hair. In her own words she was 'as plain as hell'. Ruth was not unhappy at school and managed to fulfil the unexacting demands of a prewar council education. She never learned to spell properly and she dropped her aitches. Her clearest memory of Basingstoke was a fancy dress ball to which she and her brother Granville went with their father. Granville was an ancient Briton and Ruth was an angel in a white dress with a silver-painted halo. Her father went as a horse – the rear end. Doubtless influenced by her regular attendance at a Roman Catholic Sunday School, she later recalled that at the party 'I felt ready to ascend to Heaven.'

Her mother's memory of her at this time was later reported by Mr Godfrey Winn after Ruth's conviction for murder. Writing in the now dead *Sunday Dispatch*, Mr Winn quoted Mrs Neilson as saying: 'Ruth hated us to be poor. She hated boys too at that time. That seems so strange now. But she always liked clothes and she would borrow mine and dress up in them. She wasn't like my other children. She was so very ambitious for herself. She used to say "Mum, I'm going to make something of my life." '

At fourteen Ruth left school, very willingly, and she and her family joined the great migratory tribes of wartime civilians in Britain. At first the Neilsons went to Reading, where Ruth worked as a waitress in a café. The wages and tips were the first sizeable amounts of money that Ruth ever had and every night she would go home and pour the day's tips from her bag on to the kitchen table. For a girl who was determined never to be poor and who loved clothes, it was a start. 'One day,' she told her brother Granville, 'I'll have a chain of restaurants.' The only disappointment was that money seemed to buy so little because it went so quickly. Ruth was incapable of saving, and if she saw something she must have it.

From Reading the Neilsons moved to Southwark in London, where Mr Neilson had a chauffeur's job which included a flat. It was 1941 and the Luftwaffe, narrowly beaten in their strategic aim of defeating the RAF by day, had turned to the less costly tactical terror of bombing London by night. To a girl of fifteen it was still fun – the excitement, the sense of purpose in making tea for firemen, and the pleasure of not knowing what tomorrow held – except for the certainty that the bombs would never hit you. A bomb fell very near her father and Ruth helped drag him, seriously injured, from the rubbish that had been home. She was a girl of great courage.

After the bombing the family moved to nearby No. 19 Farmers Road, Camberwell, and with her father sick Ruth had to find a job; she became a machine minder in the oxo factory at Southwark. The work bored her although she was quick and willing to learn, and she never got on with the other girls; they considered her 'stuck-up'. Ruth said they were jealous because she operated her machine with more skill. There was no real money here in such an essentially working-class cage.

In March 1942, she was admitted to St Giles Hospital with what was diagnosed as rheumatic fever. Later Ruth liked to say that she spent a year on her back in hospital living on nothing but boiled fish. Throughout her life, like many of us, Ruth found that the lie which got sympathy was always, apparently, worth telling. She was in fact discharged from the hospital on 3 May, 1942, with the welcome medical advice that dancing would aid a complete recovery.

Her brother Granville remembers his mother writing to tell him that Ruth was 'dance mad', but enthusiasm was no substitute for ability and Ruth never graduated beyond the night club shuffle. She was now sixteen, a slight girl with small ankles and tiny wrists. Her hair had gone darker while she was in hospital and her face was fresh and slightly pointed. She was five feet two inches tall and her measurements were thirty-four, twenty-four, thirty-four. She seemed an ordinary enough sort of girl.

She was ambitious, avaricious, spendthrift, brave, adaptable, quick-tempered and proud; she never forgot how the other girls in the oxo factory did not like her because she was so much 'cleverer than them'.

After Ruth left hospital, she did not return to the oxo factory. Instead she got a job as a photographer's assistant at the Lyceum Ballroom in the Strand, which was jammed with Servicemen on leave with money to spend on ordinary, well-built girls. It was at the Lyceum that she met Clare, a French Canadian soldier. She was seventeen, he was in his late twenties, good-looking and charming. He also had Canadian rates of pay. It was the ideal combination to sweep an ambitious girl off her feet, especially when marriage was proposed. Clare was a steady caller at their new address, 20 Padfield Road, and the Neilson family liked him.

Ruth loved him because he fulfilled her hopes and ambitions, and the gnawings of adolescent sex. With him she made the first break from the tea-slopped marble table tops of Brixton cafes to the well-glossed vulgarity of the Corner House and the warm intimacy of those Soho restaurants where the dirt comes off the plush under the nail of the inquiring finger. He gave her flowers, she travelled in taxis and he gave her money with the wartime generosity of insecure, well-paid soldiers dealing in a foreign currency.

Then to this ordinary girl, an ordinary thing happened. She became pregnant. This, far more than the war-time bombing and migrations, was to affect irrevocably the development of Ruth Neilson.

When Ruth discovered that she was pregnant, just after Christmas, 1944, Clare gallantly offered to fulfil his promise to marry her. Mrs Neilson, showing that continental realism which was one of her dominant traits, wrote to his commanding officer. It was just as well – Clare was married with two children in Canada.

He offered to divorce his wife and marry Ruth. Mrs Neilson, according to Granville, told him to do no such thing. Ruth, quite naturally, cried. Her mother recalls that she cried for day after day. Eventually Ruth came to terms with her disaster and sensibly got a job as a café cashier, which meant that she could work sitting down. It was her first realization that the man you trust and love can betray you while promising marriage and security.

On 15 September 1944, Clare Andria Neilson was born, a fine dark-haired boy. For her confinement, Ruth had been evacuated from London to the village of Gisland in Cumberland. After Clare was born Ruth returned home, there were no tears now and no recriminations; she displayed that extraordinary calm and apparent indifference that was one of the main strands of her character. Recalling this time, years later, she wrote: 'I did not feel that anything could hurt me any more and I had become emotionally rather cold and spent. Outwardly I was the same, I was quite cheerful and I found that I had a ready facility for making friends, but somehow in my association with men nothing touched me.' The little girl who had hated boys now had a deep contempt for men, the creatures who exploited you and then left you literally holding the baby. Granville Neilson recalls that Clare continued to visit the Neilsons and bring presents for the child, but Ruth had finished with him. She remained loyal to him and her own pride; she never revealed his name to anyone. When Ruth spoke about Clare Andria's father after the war, she always said that he was an American pilot who had been killed in action.

Clare did not desert either Ruth or his son, but continued to visit them both and pay maintenance. When the war ended and he returned to Canada the money stopped, as his own family doubtless absorbed all his civilian pay.

The day he sailed Clare sent her a big bunch of red roses. Red was the colour that she had always liked best. From Holloway she asked her mother to place red carnations and one white carnation on David Blakely's grave at Penn, Buckinghamshire.

The problem of looking after the baby and earning a living was solved when Ruth answered an advertisement for a photographer's model, 'evening work only'. The job was at the Camera Club, and the pay at a pound an hour was the best she had ever earned. Sometimes Ruth had to pose in the nude while groups of up to twenty cameramen snapped away. She wrote later: 'At first I felt frightfully embarrassed but I soon got used to it. It was a very respectable institution and the men treated me very decently. Often, after work was over, one or other of them would take me to one of the clubs for a drink.'

One of the clubs was the Court Club in Duke Street, WI. The club was near Grosvenor Square and was surrounded by the magic that Ruth had come to associate with the geographical expression, Mayfair. To her Mayfair was the social pinnacle for an ambitious girl, not a collection of expensive offices and expense account apartments.

The club was run by Mr Morris Conley, a fat man in his forties, of unrivalled unpleasantness, who also ran several other clubs in the area. Whoever controls our destinies did Ruth Neilson a singularly bad turn when he or they decided to allow Ruth into the Court Club.

On 11 December 1955, the late Duncan Webb reported in *The People*: 'Right in the centre of corruption in the West End of London stands the figure of Morris Conley.

'I hereby name him as Britain's biggest vice boss and the chief source of the tainted money that nourishes the evils of London night life.'

On 10 September, 1961, the *News of the World* carried a slightly less dramatic but equally condemning denunciation of Mr Conley.

'During three days watching policemen saw 82 men go to premises leased by a company. And they also saw two women who were known to them enter.

'Twelve telephones with ex-directory numbers were installed in the name of the company's secretary and director.

'"Eventually a raid took place," said Mr W. R. H. Sutton, prosecuting at Marylebone, London, "when the director, 59-year-old Morris Conley, of Duke Street, Westminster, admitted keeping a brothel."

'Mr Sutton said Conley was on the premises at Westbourne Terrace, Paddington, when the police arrived. Earlier he had been in or about frequently.

'"He was shown the nature of various paraphernalia one associates with these types of premises," Mr Sutton went on. "Each of the women who were known prostitutes had a client. Notices on the doors of some of the 19 flats gave girls' names."

'When charged Conley said: "I did not know what was going on." Nearly £400 in cash was in his pocket.

'Chief Inspector Geoffrey Ashdown, answering the magistrate, said he knew of four prostitutes living on the premises. "What were they being charged?" Chief Inspector Ashdown: "It varied according to the type of premises – between eight and twelve guineas a week for furnished accommodation."

'Conley was fined £100 and ordered to pay twenty-five guineas costs.'

In 1946, when Ruth Neilson was introduced to Morris Conley (Morrie to the club members), there was very little business like club business. The war was just over and ex-officers and other ranks had still to relax through their gratuities. The Black Market was nourished by controls and there was a depressing shortage of gin and whisky in the pubs. There were few shortages at Morrie's. Here the clothing coupon crooks drank with the out-of-town manufacturers, those famed Northern punters who fight for a halfpenny in Halifax but who throw their money about like drunken sailors when they are hypnotized by the dim lights of the West End clubs.

Ruth later recalled that she was flattered and impressed by Conley who spent the whole of their first meeting talking and drinking with her. By the end of the evening Conley, that shrewd trader in flesh, had realized that here was a girl, still unsophisticated and young, who would make a first-class hostess. She had a core of disenchantment.

She had recognized in Conley a man of money and power who could provide her with the commodity she wanted, escape from those dreary Brixton streets and a working life that meant going without to pay for shoe repairs and saving for months to get a frock that you only bought because that was the best you could afford.

Conley's terms were excessively beyond the £2-3 a week she had earned at the oxo factory and the temporary job at Woolworth's in Brixton. There was a basic salary of £5 a week and a ten per cent commission on the food and drinks you persuaded the customers to buy. The 'house' provided every hostess with free evening dresses as an additional fringe benefit.

It is an elementary law of the club jungle that customers who want to go to bed with you spend more money than those who just come in for a drink. You don't have to go to bed with everyone who asks you but it does help your 'take home' pay from the club; what you charge for the service depends on the sobriety and character of the mug.

Some women are sexually very vulnerable; all they need is someone to show them the way. Morrie's was the light that did not fail, ever.

Within a few weeks Ruth was taking £20 a week home. It was not only the money that was important. For the first time she was meeting 'good class' people, many of them members of otherwise respectable sections of society who found that the club's hours, 3 pm to 11 pm, enabled them to be real devils and have a drink at teatime. The pattern was locking together, Ruth was not going to be poor, she had the clothes, and she was going to make something of her life. If it entailed, as it did, becoming a prostitute who worked the clubs instead of the streets, it was unimportant, as she had never really cared for boys. It was undoubtedly hard work, for when the Court Club closed at 11 pm, Morrie liked the hostesses to move over to one of his other clubs, the Hollywood, where they entertained customers in nearby Welbeck Street until that closed around 2 am.

Ruth was popular with the customers, those insecure men who use money, not effort, to obtain women. They liked the way she talked to them in the masculine smut argot, for all her adult life she employed the four-letter language of Lawrence and the public convenience in her everyday chatter.

There were six other hostesses at the Court Club and one of them was a girl about Ruth's age called Vicki Martin, at least that was the name she chose to use in place of the prosaic Valerie Mewes, her real name. Like Ruth, Vicki came from a lower middle class home. She was born in Staines, Middlesex. Her parents were divorced when she was young and her childhood was unhappy. Like Ruth she started work at fourteen, odd jobs that included nursing, but none satisfying for an ambitious busty girl who wanted clothes and money. The crapulous Conley was the answer, and Vicki saw the Court Club as a stage post *en route* for a film career. Ruth herself had once taken singing lessons and elocution classes with the stage as an objective, but apart from teaching her not to drop her aitches when she was sober the course had been a disaster. The aitches still dropped when she was drunk or excited, and she was left with an off-key singing voice that she used to murder the molasses-like pop numbers which she adored.

Ruth went home to see baby Andy when she could, but the all-night parties and the weekends in the country clubs and horse-brass pubs in the Kent and Surrey fringes of London took most of her time. Ruth and Vicki liked to go on these beat-ups together, two tough working girls soaking what seemed to them to be the rich. A rich man by definition to a hostess is the one who will buy champagne, steak and brandy in limitless quantities on demand and pay your fee on top. From Vicki Ruth learned a catchphrase that they both used continuously: 'Gosh dear, now you've done it.' Like most catchphrases, it looks meaningless out of time and context, but to Ruth and Vicki it was a symbol of toughness in adversity, of never whining when life kicked you straight in the face. Occasionally Ruth met a man who aroused her femininity, a desire for a home, family and security. The hopes were dreams, but the money never dried up. Among the club's customers were men who either owned gown shops or who were in the wholesale or the manufacturing end of the business. It was through sleeping with one of these customers in exchange for frocks, that a meeting was engineered that was to be as important in her life as those with Clare and Conley.

One of the customers at the Court Club was a dental surgeon from Sanderstead in Surrey, George Johnston Ellis, aged forty-one, whose wife had divorced him in the previous year on the grounds of cruelty. Vera Ellis had been granted custody of the two young sons of the marriage. George Ellis was a hopeless alcoholic and could be violent when drunk. He was also a very good dentist and had made a lot of money during the war, when most of his competitors had been in the Forces and a drunken dentist was better than the toothache.

When George Ellis and Ruth Neilson met both were in a susceptible emotional state. The divorce had left George Ellis alone in his home in Sanderstead; he had an obsession with re-establishing himself in the imagined security of matrimony. For months after his wife left home he had gone from room to room switching lights on and off, pretending to the neighbours that all was well, that his wife was still there. George Ellis was a very lonely drunk.

It had not been a happy time for Ruth. Early in 1950 she became pregnant by one of her regular patrons – in fact all her life Ruth seems to have remained a good Catholic where contraception was concerned.

Whether the father was married or not is unknown; he made no offer of marriage and Ruth went to one of those obliging middle-European doctors in North London recommended to her by another girl at the club. Her pregnancy was ended in its third month and she returned to work immediately. By the early summer she was physically weary and was drinking heavily to remain the ever-gay companion that the customers expected for their money.

This is Ruth Ellis's description of her introduction to George Ellis and their courtship: 'I met George Ellis at the Court Club. I was told he was described as the mad dentist. I thought he was rather pathetic. He told such wild tales I think he really believed them. He used to spend a lot of money and was good for champagne. He seemed to have taken a liking to me. I found it easy to make him buy me champagne. One particular night [it was in June 1950] Vicki, Pat [another hostess] and I were in company with some members and George Ellis walked in, he wanted me to join him but I did not want to, he used to frighten me with his wild ravings. Vicki and I had planned to go out that night to a party. George Ellis kept pestering me so to get rid of him I said: "You go to the Hollywood and I will meet you there later." I had no intention of going there. So Vicki and I went to our party [here Ruth met the dress manufacturer and agreed to sleep with him].

'Next day I got to work at three o'clock – I was a bit late in getting in – and Vicki, Pat and I were sitting on the side and the door was wide open. It was a very hot day. The first thing Vicki said was "Guess what happened last night?" I said "Tell me slowly I don't feel so good today." Vicki said "George Ellis was razor slashed outside the Hollywood last night." I said "Oh Lord, was he? I feel dreadful, I sent him there."

'Vicki said: "Don't be silly, he always goes there, whether you told him to or not he would have gone anyway, he likes Beth" [she was the manageress]. Later on, early in the evening, George Ellis walked in wearing dark glasses and a most ugly red gash across his cheek. I felt like crying. He was looking in the mirror at the back of the bar at me. I did not know what to do, whether to go up and say I was sorry for not keeping the appointment with him. He bought some champagne and sent me a glass. He didn't seem to be bothered very much, carrying on in the same stupid manner. I felt better, I felt in his debt. I couldn't do enough for him. He asked the Manager if he could take me out to dinner. Ronnie [the Manager] asked me if I could stand it. I said "I think I ought to go." I was given permission as long as I was back at a certain time. George promised to get me back.

'In those days George Ellis always hired cars and drivers – we were driven to Purley Downs Golf Club where we had dinner, consequently [sic] it was George's Golf Club. We sat outside watching some friends of George's playing golf and we were drinking. I then got George to tell me the story of the night before. He stated he was dancing with some girl and he told her he was supposed to meet a girl here, she has not turned up, would she go to the Astor [a club] with him, the girl accepted his invitation – she was not a hostess by the way. He said goodnight to Beth [the manageress]. They went outside, the driver opened the door for them. Just as they were about to get into the car, a man came at George, George's driver ran away, I believe he was an old man. This man cut him across the face with a razor and kicked the girl on the pavement. It worked out that the man's name was [a known crook] and the girl, his girl. George Ellis was described by the newspapers as a company director [he was a director of the Crystal Palace Football Club and he resigned soon after]. The man was sentenced to four years imprisonment. I had never seen or heard of these two people in my life before.

'George got me back to the club very late.

'Ronnie [the manager] was annoyed. George Ellis spent the rest of the night at the club. I had been drinking quite a lot. George had changed his driver, he was quite young and in the club waiting. We went to the Astor after this and I was very drunk. I woke up next morning at Elmwood, Sander-stead, George's house. That day I heard the story of his wife leaving him – he told me he had gone to play golf at the Purley Downs Golf Club. When he returned, his wife and children had gone. I really felt sorry for him. He was very much in love with her.

'I spent a lot of time in his company, he took me out shopping, bought me lots of expensive things. We ate at the best places, in fact he showered me with everything. I did not get fond of him only to the extent of what he could spend on me. It was summer holiday time, so we went off to Cornwall. I did not tell Morrie [Morrie Conley, the Court Club's owner] I was going so he was rather annoyed with me walking off with one of his best customers. I think we went in June and we came back in September. I don't think Newquay would have forgotten us in a hurry. Whilst we were there we decided to go sailing one day. George and the skipper put a crate of booze on the boat. While we were sailing George and the skipper were drinking, anyway we had been out all day and night came, there I was with a drunken skipper and George well and truly tight. It was the first time I had been so long at sea in an open fishing boat. I was a bit scared, Cornwall isn't the best place to get lost at sea; it is very rocky and dangerous. One of the engines gave out, it just stopped. The skipper, in a drunken state, tried to find out what happened with no result. While this was going on George had taken the wheel; that, I knew, would be fatal. I was frozen, the little boat seemed to toss up and down and the waves seemed to be so high – the boat was leaking badly, I was bailing water out. Then the skipper discovered that he had not got any more fuel on board, also we had not got any navigation lights or compass. With this I was disgusted to think that they could start a journey like this without all the necessary things. I could not think the skipper was a Cornish fisherman and George was supposed to know something about sailing. I was an amateur. Then it started to rain, I wrapped myself in oilskins I found in the boat and hoped for the best – the sea can be very frightening in the middle of the night in an open boat, especially when you are not on any course and you haven't got a compass, so that you have no idea where you are going. The skipper and George hadn't got a clue whereabouts they were.

'I could see a lighthouse flashing on and off. I discovered later that this was because it was dangerous to go too near there because of rocks. George said to me that you had better start praying, this boat is in a bad shape. I said so am I. George was frightened and so was the skipper. I didn't care about George being frightened but when I saw the skipper worried I got worried. In the end we ran into a French fisherman laying lobster pots in the early hours of the morning, we asked him to lend us some fuel which he did and also to put us back on course. We pulled in at St Ives the three of us frozen, sick and wet. We walked into the nearest hotel and booked rooms. Explained to the management of our ordeal, our clothes were dried, we had hot baths and fell asleep. We slept all through the day – I got up first. George was ill so I arranged hot milk for him and aspirins.

'George was too ill to get to a phone so I had to make a call to Newquay to our driver and get him to put some clothes in a case and bring the car. George intended to go back by road. Anyway, the boat had to be taken back to Newquay. After a deep discussion the car was sent back and we sailed back to Newquay. When we got back to the hotel everyone knew of our adventures and it was the talk of the town for a few days.'

There is no doubt from this account as to who was the stronger character of the two. It was not the drunken, incompetent George Ellis but the deeply practical and courageous Ruth Neilson.

At the beginning of September 1950, George, who had been spending £100 a week on holiday, much of it on drink, decided to return to London. He was depressed. Physically and mentally he was in poor shape. Ruth had tired of the seaside and was hankering after club life again. George was unwilling to let her go so easily and suggested that they should spend a few days at the Selsdon Park Hotel in Surrey. Ruth agreed and while they were there George took her over to nearby Croydon airport where he hired a plane. He had a pilot's licence. It was a case of the fishing boat all over again and after they were airborne George flew the biplane upside down over South London. Nobody could say Ruth never made the same mistake twice.

The glamour was wearing off and the money was running short; the couple began long shouting scenes. For economy they decided to move to George's house in Sanderstead, a few miles away. When they went into the kitchen, George's mother was there. George was surprised and uneasy at this unexpected visitor.

George, who even at the age of forty-one, was still awed by his mother, panicked, and introduced Ruth as his wife; the car-hire driver was brought in to back up the story. His mother believed him but gave her son a sharp moment or two for not telling her that he had remarried. Ruth, who believed that George would inherit a fortune on his mother's death, said nothing.

The 'happy couple' decided to live at Sanderstead and George told the neighbours that they had just returned from their honeymoon. The rows grew in frequency and noise, mainly because Ruth objected to so much money being spent on drink. It was one thing for the mad dentist to push the champagne boat out in the clubs when she was getting a commission on the sale, but quite different when money that should have been spent on her went on rounds for anyone who happened to be at the bar. In the end George agreed to go into Warlingham Park Hospital, Surrey, for treatment for alcoholism. He also decided to sell the practice and start afresh. He was a voluntary patient at Warlingham Park from about the end of September until the middle of October 1950.

When George discharged himself from the hospital Ruth had become depressed with living on her own at Sanderstead and decided to have another holiday with fun. She chose the King's Arms Hotel at Westerham in Kent, where she and Vicki had often drunk during their weekend expeditions with men from the club. George, of course, was not cured by his stay at Warlingham and was soon back on the gin, with Ruth trying genuinely to get him to stop drinking. For Ruth they were not bad days; Vicki, Pat and the gang came down from the club and everyone agreed that even if old George did 'belt the bottle,' at least he was a professional man and he wasn't a bad catch.

Ruth was determined that George should start work again and he began to look for a practice. Years later when he spoke about this period in his life George Ellis claimed that Ruth had threatened that if he did not marry her she would turn 'the boys' on him and his two sons and get them carved up. Ruth's version, which seems the more truthful, was that George wanted to get married again because he thought it would help re-establish himself professionally. She was not in love with him but he did represent a chance of a decent home for herself and Andy, now six years old, and an insurance against a return to the club and that dreary procession of men. Many women have married for less honest motives and George knew about Andy and her past.

They were married at the Register Office in Tonbridge, Kent, on 8 November 1950. Ruth described her father's occupation as 'professional musician', and George gave his father's as 'wholesale fish merchant'.

Again the reasons given by the newly-weds for what

happened differ. The unquestioned fact is that the next day George returned to Warlingham Park, according to him in order to escape from Ruth who had terrorized him by her threats of the razor-slashers that she apparently had on call. Ruth's explanation is less dramatic. She had seen George's doctor before she decided to marry and he had recommended that George should take a really serious cure for the drink. Ruth agreed that she would marry him if George went to Warlingham.

From the hospital George wrote to a Southampton dentist, Mr Ronald Morgan, who owned several practices in the district. He was careful to write on notepaper that gave no indication that he was in a mental hospital, and it was agreed that he could start work in the New Year.

George, again a voluntary patient, discharged himself from the hospital and they moved the furniture from Sanderstead to the four-bedroomed house at Warsash that went with the job.

The story they told the Morgans was plausible. They were just back from their honeymoon and George had not practised for some time as the result of a nervous breakdown occasioned by overwork during the war. Ruth was frank about her time as a club hostess and George explained that he had got the razor scar on his cheek after a gallant attempt to rescue Ruth from thugs who had set on her one night at a club.

Ruth too was making concessions to professional life. She had abandoned the heavy make-up she normally wore, only using now a dab of powder and a little lipstick. Her hair, although still dyed blonde, was tied in a pony tail. They appeared a suited couple, the young woman of twenty-four who had married the florid, charming man of forty-one. Neither of them drank and the Morgans were delighted to have found someone so suitable for the practice. Most of George's work was at the Warsash surgery but he and Mr Morgan also attended at two other surgeries, one in Botley and the other in Bitterne Road, Southampton.

It was the first time Ruth had had a home of her own and Mrs Morgan recalls that Ruth seemed quite house-proud. It was not long before things started to go wrong.

The 'cure' that George had taken at Warlingham proved as temporary as all the others, and after a few weeks' sobriety he was a regular at the 'Rising Sun' at Warsash. Here, with the embarrassing insecurity of the alcoholic, he bought everyone a drink. The rows began again at home and soon became public. The dinner dance given by the Southampton branch of the British Dental Association at the Polygon Hotel was one of the local status symbols of the year and naturally the Ellises and the Morgans made up a table.

Ruth was wearing a draped chiffon dress that left one shoulder bare. She danced occasionally, for despite the lessons in her teens and her time as a hostess she was still awkward on her feet. George saw little of his wife as he was boisterously immovable at the bar. Later, while Ruth was talking to a group of men, he left the bar to announce that they were leaving at once. George had borrowed the Morgans' second car, a small Fiat, to drive to the Polygon and the row continued in the car back to Warsash. The bickering ran to a predictable pattern; George told Ruth to get out of the car and walk home so Ruth got out and started to walk down a country lane in heavy rain, wearing black satin shoes. George drove on only to return a few minutes later. There was the usual 'Get in' and 'I won't' until George dragged her in and they went home to continue the row. There was a fight and next day Ruth packed a bag with clothes for herself and Andy and went home to mother, at 7 Herne Hill Road, Brixton. Predictably she returned within two days.

In many marriages a row ensures the peace of emotional exhaustion; with Ruth it only renewed her feeling that George would be like all the other men and try to exploit her. There was no relaxation in tension. What happened in the next few months was a rehearsal of the pattern of events that was to be repeated four years later and precede the killing of David Blakely.

During the six months that George and Ruth had lived together in Cornwall and Surrey she had always known where he was; the rows had been over money and George's drunkenness. Now they were married, the rows over money and drink continued but to this sufficiently explosive mixture was added the dynamite of jealousy. It was in order, as the incident at the dance had shown, for Ruth to surround herself with men and flirt, but George had only to speak to another woman and it was adultery. Boredom had a part in these outbursts, for Ruth was lonely at Warsash. Her neighbours were old and her only companion was Mrs Bourne the daily, who came in to clean; Mrs Morgan lived too far away for easy social relations, although she would have been willing to have seen more of Ruth. Allowing for the boredom and the comparative shortage of money since George was paying his first wife alimony of £8 a week and spending more than that a week on gin, it is indisputable that Ruth Ellis was a woman obsessed by a quite unreasoning jealousy.

If a woman patient rang to fix an appointment and George answered the phone he was arranging a secret meeting. If he worked late at the Botley or Southampton practices he was having an affair with his nurse, or a patient. Mrs

Morgan was often phoned by Ruth to discover whether George had left, or whether he was working late. On these occasions, she spoke in a high, excited voice.

Her suspicions were aggravated by the time it often took George to get home by the indifferent bus service. He had no car and sometimes was unable to borrow Mrs Morgan's Fiat. It was when the Fiat was in a garage at Warsash that another of the physical fights of the marriage occurred. George arrived at the garage and found that the car was not ready, so he naturally went to the 'Rising Sun'. An hour or so later he returned to the garage to be told that Mrs Ellis had been asking for him there. He thought there was some emergency at home and returned straightaway, but the house was empty. Some time later Ruth appeared in a car and explained that she had hired it to go to Botley to look for her George. Questioned by him, she admitted that she had driven to the house of one of his patients with whom she suspected him of having an affair, but as there was nobody in, and no sign of the Fiat in the street outside, she had come home. George, who had been drinking at home while she was out, beat her up badly when she returned. It did no good and the accusations of infidelity became a daily affair. Sometimes Ruth and Andy would leave for Brixton and then return soon afterwards. Like many a loving daughter Ruth found a few days at home an inducement to rejoin her husband.

By April the marriage was obviously rocky. Ruth had called the police twice after George had returned home drunk and violent. Once he had kicked down the front door when Ruth had locked it against him. On her side, the nagging and jealousy increased and she regularly hired cars to visit her husband unexpectedly at work in the hope as she told him 'of catching you at it with one of those bloody stuck-up patients'.

At home she continued the barrage, calling him 'a drunken old has-been from a lunatic asylum'. In return George dubbed her 'a bloody bitch from Brixton' and infuriated her by hiring cars to go up to London and visit the Astor Club.

It could not last, and the heavy drinking affected George's efficiency as a dentist. One April afternoon, George's receptionist telephoned Mr Morgan to ask if he knew where Mr Ellis was, as it was now four o'clock and Mr Ellis had promised to be back by 2.30 pm; there were about seven patients waiting. Mr Morgan did not know where his assistant could be, but the mystery was ended when half an hour later George phoned from the Isle of Wight to ask the receptionist to cancel all his appointments as 'it was such a lovely day I decided to pop over to Cowes'. As there was a bar on the steamer that was open for the trip, it was obvious that George had left the pubs in Southampton at closing time and decided on the voyage as a means of carrying on with the gin. Although Ruth refused to believe it, drink was the only outside interest in George Ellis's life.

The Cowes episode was the last straw for Mr Morgan, and George was told politely that he was fired.

George, of course, told everyone that he had given Mr Morgan a week's notice, but the villagers at Warsash who knew of his drinking habits, were unimpressed. So were his patients, who for months had been forced to inhale the stench of the cough sweets that George chewed in the daytime to mask the odour of the gin.

In May the Ellises left Warsash and went to stay with George's mother in Bettws-y-Coed in Wales. Before he left Warsash, George had inquired about working for Mr W.J. Littleton, a dental surgeon with a practice in Cliff Road, Newquay, Cornwall. While he was at Warlingham Park

Hospital over Christmas 1950, Mr Littleton had been one of the dentists to whom George had either written or telephoned asking for work. Fortunately for him the Newquay job was still open and he got it.

The stay with George's mother did not reconcile the couple and once more Ruth decided to go back to her mother in London while George went on his own to Newquay. It was about the sixth time since their marriage that she had left her husband. George stayed in alcoholic bachelordom at the Beachcroft Hotel, but he was not alone for long. Somehow Ruth had discovered where he was living and telephoned him suggesting a reconciliation. According to George, Ruth promised to behave herself and not to worry him either at work or off duty with allegations of infidelity.

By now Ruth had discovered that she was pregnant, so a reconciliation with George was obviously the best short-term solution. He sent her the fare and she joined him at the hotel.

There was no peace in Torquay. George did not give up drinking, nor Ruth her irrational jealousy. Within days she was accusing him of affairs with patients and staff, without proof in either case. After some weeks in Newquay, George told Ruth that he wanted to go to Southampton to see the local inspector of taxes. He proposed to go via London. It was certainly true, but Ruth immediately accused him of having arranged an assignation with one of his former patients either in London or Southampton. There was the inevitable row and Ruth said that as in any case she was leaving him and returning to her parents she would accompany him on the overnight train. By this Ruth would get her fare paid to London and would also be able to see if there was anyone meeting George on the sleeper or not.

Not surprisingly there was no romantic encounter either

on the train or at Paddington, but Ruth insisted on accompanying George to Waterloo to see that he caught the train for Southampton. At Waterloo she asked George for £5 and said that she would go home by tube, and a relieved George watched her descend the Underground steps. He then caught the Southampton train and was about to take up drinking stations in the dining car, when Ruth appeared in the compartment and announced that she had caught the train at the last moment. She told George that she was still not satisfied that he was not going to Southampton to meet a woman.

Nothing more romantic than HM Inspector of Taxes materialized at Southampton and they returned to Waterloo that evening. George had drunk through most of his money during the day and was faced with paying his wife's fare back to Newquay. As British Railways refused to take cheques for passenger fares in those days, he decided that the only thing to do was to go and have a drink somewhere where they would accept a cheque. Together they took a cab to Ruth's old club and cashed a cheque; later they caught the night train from Paddington.

Foiled in Southampton, Ruth continued to look for adultery in Newquay and again resorted to her Warsash trick of arriving unexpectedly at the surgery. There was a scene at the Great Western Hotel when Ruth threw a glass of orange juice over George after he had shouted that she was a Brixton girl and that he had married beneath him. In times of trouble George inevitably increased his drinking, and if that failed to bring peace, he retreated to his base hospital at Warlingham Park. Drink having failed, George once more decided to become a voluntary patient. By this time Ruth was about four months pregnant, which increased the tension under which they were both living.

Ruth frequently visited the hospital where she accused George of improper relations with the female staff and other patients. As usual her language was direct and expressive. On one visit she pointed to a woman patient with whom George was friendly, saying: 'So that's the old bag you're getting it with here.' She threatened to report George to the Dental Board, not only for his conduct in the hospital, but because he was 'plotting' to bring up 'that bag from Newquay'.

George, who had already threatened his wife with legal proceedings, tried to get her to sign a document apologizing for her past behaviour and withdrawing her accusations of infidelity. Ruth refused to sign, and continued to visit her husband, mainly to get money to keep her while she was living at home with her mother. By the autumn the couple were exchanging solicitors' letters, those snowflakes that precede a matrimonial blizzard. George refused to see his wife at the hospital unless there was a witness present, a condition that Ruth refused to fulfil.

On 2 October, 1951, Ruth entered the maternity ward at Dulwich Hospital where she had a 7 lb girl, Georgina, after a difficult confinement (this was a medical, not subjective, opinion). George did not help by ignoring the event, although he did provide a layette for the baby in addition to allowing Ruth £4 a week. George left Warlingham Park for Warrington in Lancashire without telling Ruth where he was going, and instructed his solicitors to suggest that the baby should be adopted. Ruth was seriously ill after the birth of Georgina and spent a fortnight in hospital before going home with the baby, and whatever their differences in the past it is indisputable that her husband was behaving badly.

Ruth refused to give up the child and when she registered Georgina's birth at Dulwich she concealed that the father's residence at the time of birth was a mental home, and gave his address as 7 Herne Hill Road, Lambeth, SE24, the Neilson home. George, though ignorant of this white lie, responded by refusing to pay the bill for a pram and by publishing the foolish husband's delusion of revenge, a notice in the local press repudiating his wife's right to pledge his credit.

Even Ruth could see that the marriage was over and in November George applied to the High Court for an order to file a petition for divorce on the grounds of cruelty. The application was made although the couple had not been married for three years, the period of trial and error that the law demanded before disaster was legally definite. The judge who considered the application refused it, and advised the couple to seek a reconciliation. With a baby to support and no home of her own, Ruth was willing to live with George again but he refused. It was less than a year since they had married.

To Ruth it proved that marriage was as unsatisfactory as any other form of relationship with men; it was clear that the only way to treat men was strictly as the temporary and changeable providers of cash, clothes and comfort.

She was twenty-five and financially was no better off than she had been as a waitress at the beginning of the war, and now she had two children to support. The only decent item in the wardrobe of this girl who loved clothes was a black tailor-made which she wore with a white silk blouse. Emotionally her pattern was more defined. She had married George, on her own admission, to provide a home for herself and Andy. She had been sorry for him after the slashing but love had no part in the marriage, and there had been the additional inducement that Ruth believed George would inherit a fortune when his mother, who was then nearly seventy, died. For months while she was living with George before they married she was able to view him dispassionately, but once he became hers through marriage, she revealed an unexpected irrational jealousy and possessiveness. It was this almost mad jealousy, as much as the drink, that made George Ellis a violent husband. With people with whom she was not emotionally involved Ruth was amazingly controlled and calm in difficult situations. Few suspected her violent temper, a trait she knew was bad for business. In her relations with a man with whom she was deeply involved she was a woman who never knew when to shut up. It is also true that most of the men she knew gave her plenty to complain about.

The crisis would come when 'love' was added to her unreasoning jealousy and triggered an emotional H-Bomb.

George remained in hiding although he agreed to pay £4 a week to support Ruth and Georgina.

It was clearly useless to harry George any further and Ruth, with her customary realism, cut her losses and decided to return to work. Fortunately there was Mum to look after the two children and if nothing else had come out of the marriage with George she had been able to give Andy a name, even unofficially. Henceforth he was known as Andria Ellis.

In trouble, George retreated to Warlingham Park. Ruth's move was to get in touch with Morrie Conley. 'Hostessing' was the only trade she knew, and he was delighted to hear from her. She had been told by the hospital to rest as much as possible and to continue attending for treatment following the difficult confinement. She began to work before she was fit, but continued to visit the gynaecological clinic until June 1952; although advised to return for further treatment, she later failed to keep an appointment. She never went back because she was too busy at Carroll's, the new name for the old Court Club where she had worked before her marriage to George Ellis. Now, furnished with a restaurant, cabaret and dancing it was open until 3 am, mainly for 'tired' businessmen too weary for sleep; other customers included several old-established clients of that other moderately exclusive club, West End Central in Savile Row.

It was one of the happiest times of her life. She was wanted and momentarily admired by many. There was a banker from Persia, an oil expert from Canada, an industrialist from Norway, and a tycoon from Switzerland who, acumen blunted by passion, signed his notes 'always your naughty Norbert'.

Vicki Martin was still trying to get into films and still discovering that producers were always ready to buy you dinner to discuss your career, but it inevitably turned out that your destiny was not on the screen but between sheets. Still, Vicki soldiered on and smoked cigars for publicity pictures in the hope that someone would equate this with her conviction that she really had acting talent. This was Vicki's year for going platinum blonde, so Ruth did the same. They lent each other money and never paid it back, they got hung over together, it was a grand whoring world.

Sometimes the other girls asked her if she wished she were back in Warsash. Ruth made them realize how fortunate they were in London by inevitably repeating: 'Do you know that in that bloody hick dump you can't even buy a pair of nylons?'

Since the break with George, Ruth had ostensibly been living at home with Andy, Georgina and her parents. The Neilsons had moved yet again to No. 11 Lucien Road, Tooting Bec. It was, to Ruth, another permutation of the Neilsons' wanderings around the grey prison area of South London. In her jargon she 'wanted out'.

'Out' was provided by Morrie Conley, tyre-lipped, jowled, and conspicuously avaricious. He arranged that

Ruth should move into Flat 4, Gilbert Court, a block in Oxford Street, owned by Morrie's wife, Hannah. Here, doubtless unknown to the faithful Hannah and other residents, Morrie housed many of his hostesses, charging them high rents which they paid out of their call-girl earnings.

Both Morrie and Ruth found Flat 4 convenient; he could call when he liked, for in his fashion he was fond of her. She had a better base for her call-girl enterprises. She was pleased too with the phone number Mayfair 8534, nothing common or Brixton about that. Of course there was Morrie; it was essential to be friendly with him, since unfriendly girls found that the thoughtful Morrie kept a set of duplicate keys to their flats and they would return home to find all the frocks in their wardrobes slashed and ruined. For Ruth, Morrie was a fact of life, like sore throats or measles; you could live with it.

Life went on in its uncomplicated haze – getting up at noon, eating too many chocolates, drinking too much gin, and never making quite enough money to pay for the compulsive spending on clothes.

Just before Christmas 1952 Ruth complained to the other hostesses that she thought she had gastric 'flu. Brandy just made her feel sick. The pain grew and she called her doctor who satisfied himself that it apparently was neither pregnancy nor appendicitis. Fortunately he was not one of those medical men who believe that most pain will vanish under the soothing influence of aspirin, a good night's sleep and a dose of salts. The doctor was also not afraid to say that he did not know what was wrong with her and he sent Ruth off to the Middlesex Hospital. Here specialists diagnosed ectopic pregnancy, the condition where the foetus begins to grow, not in the womb, but in one of the Fallopian tubes. If this condition is not immediately and skilfully treated the patient could die. Ruth was in hospital for over a fortnight and was advised to rest when she was discharged. This time she decided to do what the doctors said. It was pointed out to her that going back to work too early after the birth of Georgina had contributed to her present illness.

The girls from the club came to see her. The ward was full of expensive spring flowers from Betty, Michele, Cathy and Kitty. Some of the boyfriends looked in and others wrote.

By April she was back at the Club. A photograph of the party given to celebrate her return shows the empty, lecherous faces of the regular clientele. Ruth is wearing a faintly Lesbian outfit of a severe white jacket whose neck is filled by a silk scarf knotted in that strange square-fronted way then favoured by homosexuals. In one hand she has a long holder into which she has clamped a cigarette. The other hand rests on a bottle-bedecked table. She has the rather surprised, wide-pupilled look of the slightly drunk. Her partner, like all the other men in the picture, is fleshy, with well-oiled hair; he looks sexually expectant. His left hand is round Ruth's waist, the fingers touching her breast. He was the sort of man for whom Ruth kept printed cards that he could take away to show to the other 'lads' at the office. The cards carried slightly off-colour doggerel like:

> Why women over 40 are preferred.
> THEY DON'T YELL!
> THEY DON'T TELL!
> THEY DON'T SWELL!
> and they are as
> GRATEFUL AS HELL!

There was no extra charge for the cards.
She had other cards that she gave to less straightforward

clients. These advertised a firm specializing in the handtailoring of model rainwear for those whose sexual awareness can only be aroused by memories of the rubber sheeting of their nursery days. Ruth got commission from all the customers she introduced.

To encourage perverts she kept hand-drawn, highly-coloured sets of out-of-perspective pornographic pictures painted on white cardboard. Some of these dealt with the relations between the Lesbian headmistress of a girls' school and her pupils. Perhaps Ruth was a Lesbian, as she knew plenty of them, but there is no direct proof.

The summer and autumn of 1953 were financially boom times for Ruth Ellis. One of her clients gave her about £400 after she had been on holiday with him. Ruth told everyone it was £1,000. Years later Ruth would produce the cancelled cheques as proof that someone really had given her the money. The gift made her temporarily independent; she went out more and spent less time at the club. Her great satisfaction was to go there with her boyfriend and drink without worrying about the commission from Morrie for inducing the mug to buy as much champagne as possible. Over money it was she who was the mug. All the other girls, and Vicki, looked on her as an 'easy touch' for a fiver, and she was. Then there was her own lust for clothes which was never satisfied. By September the money was almost gone; a cheque drawn on the 18th in favour of a dress shop was marked 'Refer to drawer' but the bank honoured it on representation.

# 3

# David Blakely

It was clear that Ruth would have to start work again. During the summer she had made new friends who interested her more than the paunchy businessmen and manufacturers with whom she normally mixed and slept. The new 'gang' were motor racing drivers who had decided to add Carroll's to the Steering Wheel Club in Brick Street as a place for approved drinking. Their leader was Mike Hawthorn, who was six feet two inches tall, a rather loose-lipped, blond young man, of twenty-three.

Hawthorn was killed five years later when his Jaguar skidded 133 yards after it hit a bollard on the Guildford by-pass. In the entourage that followed him while he was alive there were two young men, David Blakely and Desmond Cussen.

Hawthorn set the standard that Blakely followed of hard drinking and hard driving, and an intense but rootless association with women; the whole ending in sudden death. The two were not friends, and were only united by a community of interest in racing, driving cars at excessive speed on the roads, and by being on drinking terms with the same young men and women of their set.

This is Ruth's description of her first meeting with David Blakely, when he was twenty-four and she nearly twenty-seven. It was not the heady, exciting stuff that Jim Eilbeck had dreamed of when he bought the story for *Woman's Sunday Mirror*. We did our best with it, but Jim never liked it; 'No champagne touch,' he said.

'I was at Carroll's Club, as a guest this time, with the motor-racing boys, including Desmond Cussen, whom I had only just met, when in strolled David wearing an old coat and flannel trousers. I did not like his manner from the start, I thought he was too hoity-toity by far.

'He greeted the other lads in a condescending manner and was offhand in his acceptance of the proffered drink. He lounged on the bar with his back to the other girls and started making derogatory remarks, referring to the Club as "a den of vice" and jerking his head towards the hostesses and saying "I suppose these are the so-called hostesses" and so on.

'My hackles began to rise and I turned to the other boys and in a plainly audible voice so that he could hear I said "Who is that pompous little ass?" He turned to me and said: "I suppose you are another of them?"

'I said, "No, as a matter of fact I am an old has-been." He finished his drink and said "Come on boys, let's get out of this sink of iniquity" and lounged out of the bar. I was definitely not impressed with Mr Blakely. I thought he was too big for his boots.'

David Moffett Drummond Blakely was born on 17 June 1929, at the Oakdale Nursing Home, No. 33 Collegiate Crescent, Sheffield, at that time the city's best nursing home.

His father, Dr John Blakely from Glasgow, lived and practised in a large sombre house, No. 203 School Road, in the hilly Sheffield suburb of Crookes.

David was the youngest of the doctor's four children. His elder brothers were Derek Andrew Gustav and John Brian;

there was one sister, Maureen, to whom David was particularly attached. The children had a nanny who was devoted to young David; he in turn loved her deeply and always spoke of her with pleasure and treated her with warmth and consideration. He was fond of his mother, but she seemed to him a more remote figure than 'Nanny'. The neighbours who still remember the Blakely family agree that David was 'a happy child'.

His parents were not often so happy. Dr Blakely was brusque, fond of golf and by inclination a home bird. His wife Annie is remembered locally as 'more society than the doctor, a smart sophisticated woman fond of a gay time'.

When Dr Blakely put up his plate in Crookes after the First World War he became the most popular doctor in the district. He had the old-fashioned family doctor's air of curt, infallible mystery that has disappeared with the Health Service. His patients respected and loved this tall, dark and distinguished-looking man, and there was no nonsense about 'reporting him to the Executive' if he was half-an-hour late for little Johnny's high temperature.

His patients were lower middle class, which meant that in the England of the thirties they were mostly employed, when lucky, in rather ill-paid white-collar jobs or in skilled trades in Sheffield. Often they were so poor that, like their counterparts throughout the land, they could not afford a doctor. They were fortunate to have Dr John, as he was known locally, for he would never refuse to treat a patient and would allow them to pay his bill at the rate of sixpence a week. His patients' loyalty was unmistakably shown in the winter of 1934.

On 10 February a small news item appeared in the *Daily Herald* under the headlines:

## DYING WAITRESS RIDDLE DRIVEN
## HOME THEN CAR VANISHED

The story of a dying girl being driven home in a motor car which disappeared was told at the inquest yesterday at Sheffield on Phyllis Staton, aged 25, an unemployed waitress who died in hospital. The inquest was adjourned.

The girl's father said that she had been keeping company with a professional man for two years. In the middle of January she left home and he received two letters with a Sheffield postmark but no address.

On Saturday last, he added, the girl returned home and fell on the floor saying: 'Oh Mother I shall die.' The father rushed outside and saw a motor car being driven away.

The girl's sister said that when she asked who had brought her back she said 'The Doc.'

On 21 February the *Daily Telegraph* carried a longer news story under the headlines:

## DOCTOR & WAITRESS ALLEGED
## STATEMENT IN MURDER CHARGE

Dr John Blakely, 49, of School Road, Sheffield, appeared on remand at Sheffield yesterday charged with the murder of Phyllis Staton, 25, an unemployed waitress. A further charge was preferred of unlawfully applying a drug for a certain purpose.

Mr J.W. Chant, prosecuting, said that during the past eighteen months the woman had been continually in the company of Dr Blakely. She left home on 15 January and her parents did not see anything more of her until 3

February when there was a knock on the back door of the house and the girl fell in. Dr Blakely was then seen driving away in his car. The woman died in hospital the next day from acute septicaemia.

Detective Superintendent Bristow produced a statement alleged to have been made by Dr Blakely in which he said that he had given the woman some drugs but denied having carried out an illegal operation. He admitted intimacy with the girl but said that she had been with other men and that she had picked upon him because of his being better off than the others.

Superintendent Bristow in answer to Mr F.W. Scorah, defending, said that he could find no evidence to support any allegation about Miss Staton's relations with men.

Dr James Clark, medical superintendent of Sheffield City General Hospital, said there was no evidence of any illegal operation or the taking of drugs. Asked if it was possible for a medical man to procure an abortion without leaving any evidence the doctor replied 'Yes, it is.'

The hearing was adjourned until today.

On 22 February the *Daily Telegraph* reported:

## DOCTOR ACQUITTED ON MURDER CHARGE

After hearing the speech for the defence the Sheffield magistrates last night dismissed the charges brought against Dr John Blakely, 49, of the murder of an unemployed waitress Phyllis Staton, 25, and of supplying a certain drug to the girl knowing it to be intended for unlawful use.

The presiding magistrate said the evidence was so weak that no jury would convict.

For the prosecution it was alleged that Dr Blakely had procured a miscarriage in such a way that a post-mortem would not implicate him and that a drug had been used.

For the defence, Mr F.W. Scorah said that the miscarriage was perfectly normal. There was no evidence that the accused had anything to do with it.

Reading these cuttings nearly thirty years later, no one can fault the Sheffield magistrates' opinion that no jury would convict on that evidence. The Crown's case was hopeless from the start. Dr John had admitted nothing damaging in his statement and the principal witness, Miss Staton, was dead. What does not appear to have been questioned was that Miss Staton had been Dr John's mistress for at least eighteen months.

The effect of the trial on the doctor's practice was nil. Whatever the patients thought they kept to themselves and with Northern judgment reckoned that it was the sort of thing that might happen to any man, and it was bloody hard luck if it happened to a man who turned out in the middle of a winter's night to treat your sick and let you pay the bill at sixpence a week.

David Blakely was almost five when his father appeared on this charge of murder and it is most improbable at the time that he either heard or knew of the case. But he did find out about it later and told Ruth Ellis. She, with the realism of the Southern working class, and the memory of her own abortions, felt neither shock nor disgust at the story.

It was clearly an incident that was unlikely to strengthen the marriage of David's parents. David told Ruth that Phyllis Staton was one of the major frictions in the breakup, which came early in the Second World War. On 24 May,

1940, Mrs Blakely was granted a decree nisi for the dissolution of her marriage 'by reason that since the celebration thereof the said Respondent [Dr Blakely] had been guilty of adultery'. No woman was named in the suit.

David was nearly eleven when his parents were divorced. Later, when he talked about it with friends, he recalled the event with sadness. The emotional security which should envelop a boy of eleven had gone. He was devoted to his father and fond of his mother. Mrs Blakely was awarded the custody of the children and the divorce became absolute on 2 December, 1940.

On 4 February, 1941, Mrs Blakely remarried. David's stepfather was Humphrey Wyndham Cook, the wealthy son of a wholesale draper. Before the Second World War, Humphrey Cook was one of Britain's best-known racing car drivers. He was forty-seven, the same age as his new wife. He had also been married before and was divorced.

For the Register Office wedding at Caxton Hall in London Mrs Blakely gave her address as the Hyde Park Hotel, London, and Humphrey Cook gave his as 38 Upper Brook Street, WI. This time Annie Blakely, *née* Moffett, had changed her mind about the profession followed by her father John Moffett (deceased). At the 1913 wedding to Dr John Blakely at Ballynahinch she gave her father's profession as 'horse dealer'. At the Caxton Hall wedding it was given as 'of independent means'.

The girl from Ballynahinch had no difficulty in fitting into the Mayfair living of Humphrey Cook. Her suits came from Michael, her jewellery from Cartier and Boucheron. Those who knew her after the war recall that she was well-built, of medium height (five feet five inches) with grey hair and blue eyes. She had an easy, Irish charm.

Like most families the war split the Blakelys, and the two elder sons, Derek and Brian, were in the Forces. David went to Shrewsbury, a second division public school in a small Midlands town on the borders of North Wales. Fortunately, the Blakely children liked their mother's new husband and Humphrey and David found that they had one shared, absorbing interest, motor racing cars. Above all, in the holidays, there was always Nanny. She provided an understanding and loving anchorage in the world of war and disrupted homes.

At Shrewsbury David showed no intellectual distinction; his only deep interest was in racing cars, a subject not on the school curriculum. He left school after the war with no power of analysis—all his short adult life David Blakely could never engage in a sustained, reasoned argument, and he was sullen and dogmatic in debate. At Shrewsbury he developed a literary taste that regarded the Saint books by Leslie Charteris as sufficient intellectual test for any man. David was no testimonial for the public school as a place where young minds are nurtured.

On the other hand, his public school background helped him to get a commission in the Highland Light Infantry when he did his National Service. After he was demobbed there was the question of earning a living. It was difficult to know what to do with a lad who was really only interested in racing cars. Humphrey Cook understood very well from his experience with the ERA that motor racing is a most expensive interest. He decided that David should have a trade and arranged for him to become a trainee at the fashionable Hyde Park Hotel in Knightsbridge. It was here that Mrs Cook had stayed before her wedding and the family were well known to the management. David was to receive fifty shillings a week from the hotel and an allowance of £5 a week from his mother. Ultimately David would be the manager of a first-class hotel, or perhaps Mr Cook would set him up in his own hotel.

It was a thoughtful move by Mr Cook and on the surface appeared to be in David's interest. The fact that the Little Club was two minutes' walk across the road was a matter of no importance at the time.

David disliked the hotel business; the hours were long, the money indifferent and insufficient. This shortage of cash, he explained to his mother, prevented him entertaining the sort of girl she was always urging him to meet, the débutante. In reality David had little sympathy with these unsophisticated products of the plutocracy and aristocracy. They were useless to David and he to them, for despite his commission in the Army David had little confidence or ability to cope with life; he was always looking for an older woman to teach him what the world was all about. It was this basic lack of masculinity—fostered by the security of those two masculine spheres, the public school and the Army, that kept him away from girls of his own social and economic class rather than the financial handicap of being a trainee at the Hyde Park Hotel.

# 4

# The Findlaters and Lover Boy

David Blakely was of medium height, five feet nine inches, and slim, weighing eleven stone. David's brown eyes and his long almost silky eyelashes were characteristics that women who knew him instantly recalled. He had the easy, good manners that are so important for success with women.

His voice was of a pleasant pitch; in it there was none of the metallic presumption of the public school and the barrack square.

With this went an almost complete Irish inability to arrive for an appointment on time. He was, according to a man friend, 'a dead unreliable bastard'. To the older girl-friend, David was the little boy who had got lost on the way; to be scolded, kissed and forgiven.

Women loved to mother him and this was more rewarding to them than any sexual intimacy that resulted; according to women who slept with him, David Blakely was an indifferent partner. Men who believe that women must always be sexually satisfied to be happy are obviously students of textbooks rather than life.

The most lasting of these girlfriends was a theatre usherette, a feather-brained platinum blonde with tiny wrists and ankles, who never nagged if David disappeared for weeks while he was having an affair with other women. The hotel of course was a wonderful recruiting ground for his type of women, staying alone in London for a few days. They had the money, the experience and the sexual drive of boredom; David had the youth, good looks and charm. When he was working at the reception desk, as part of the thorough training given to him at the hotel, David was wonderfully placed to exploit his charm in return for free meals and drinks. Those who feel moral indignation about this way of life might ponder whether it is more unworthy than sucking up to relatives you hate in the expectation of inheriting money, or being a 'yes-man' and 'nodder' at work in order to get promotion.

Older women too, were more tolerant of his cowardice when he was away from the racing track where fear left him. In clubs and pubs he was for ever starting arguments and running away.

One night at the Steering Wheel Club a rather drunken Blakely, who was out for the evening with another racing driver, Cliff Davis, went up to Mike Hawthorn and put ice cubes down his neck. Just to add to the undergraduate humour of it all, he then squirted Hawthorn with soda water from a syphon. Hawthorn, understandably, was not amused, and struck at Blakely who scuttled in fear. The blow knocked off Davis's glasses, and Davis, who like many people, had an uncontrollable reaction if anyone touches their glasses, hit Hawthorn. The scene ended with apologies and drinks all round.

Racing cars were as important to David as women and even when he was a fifty shillings a week trainee at the Hyde Park Hotel, he managed to get enough money to attend meetings near London and to borrow money from his family to run a sports car, which he entered for races that gave him experience but no victories. Often he would drive to Sheffield to see his father; the years had increased the tender relationship between father and son. Even so, David never ceased to be affected by the break-up of his home and as Carole Findlater, who was one of his friends, puts it: 'How he needed family, my goodness how that boy needed it.'

David first met Carole Findlater in 1951 and again, as so often in the Ruth Ellis story, this was one of those occasions when an ordinary event has an extraordinary and violent finale.

In 1951 a Mr Findlater advertised for sale an ancient Alfa-Romeo car and gave the address of a flat in Colet Gardens, Hammersmith, a road of Victorian villas that flanked the playing fields of St Paul's School, that suburban Prudential Assurance building. The advertisement was answered by a man whose name Mrs Findlater has long forgotten, but he was accompanied by a polite, well-mannered young man whose name she remembers clearly, David Blakely.

Mrs Carole Findlater was twenty-seven when she met David Blakely, and he was twenty-three. Her husband, Anthony Seaton Findlater, was twenty-nine and the marriage, which was neither happy nor successful, ended in divorce eighteen months after the death of David Blakely. Carole, unlike her husband, was Jewish and her parents, the Sonins, had come to England as Czarist refugees at the beginning of the century. Albert Sonin, a manufacturer's agent, was an honourable man who kept his family in middle-class comfort.

During the war Carole became Leading Aircraftwoman 2130389 in the Women's Auxiliary Air Force where she drove a radio truck. It was not a bad war for Carole; there was a sense of purpose in the WAAF, excitement and boyfriends. In her spare time she studied Russian. While Carole was serving at the RAF station at Sawbridgeworth in Hertfordshire, she met a very good-looking young Sergeant, also in the RAF, who was working in the instruments section. His name was Anthony Findlater and he was delighted to ask the slim, dark-haired WAAF to a Sergeants' Mess Party. It was a typical wartime boy-meets-girl affair and soon the dashing Sergeant, who kept a sheath knife in his sock, was posted to Italy and Carole imagined that it was over. However, he wrote to her and when he returned to England at the end of the war they began meeting frequently. Carole was delighted with Anthony, for to her he was so ideally English, well-mannered, an ex-public schoolboy from Hurstpierpoint, and wonderfully unworried by having very little money although his family were reasonably well-off.

Anthony Findlater had been a student before the war in automobile engineering; to him, like David Blakely, cars were a way of life, an obsession that could transcend women, money, home, drink, and all the common interests of uncommitted men. Like David he had not been bright at his public school. His father, Seaton Findlater, was a member of the Presbyterian Dublin Findlater family, who had built up a prosperous grocery business in this Roman Catholic sea. Seaton was sent to England for the first stage of his education at Harrow but returned to Dublin as an undergraduate at Trinity College. Seaton went back to England and became one of the better known prewar racing drivers; he was also a competent and successful motor-car engine designer and the family settled in Lower Wick, a suburb of Worcester. Findlater senior refused to encourage his son's ambition to become a racing driver. Father and son did not get on. Seaton regarded Anthony as an idiot, and he repeatedly told Carole 'I can't see what a pretty, intelligent girl like you can see in that bloody fool son of mine.'

Bloody fool or not, Anthony was in love with Carole and she with him and soon after the war they were married at Kensington Register Office. Anthony was twenty-four and she was twenty-two. Like thousands after the peace they had no immediate jobs to which to return; the situation was not worrying for lovers. Realistically, Carole told Anthony not to fret. 'I can earn,' she said. Like many quick-witted people with no particular training for anything, Carole had been a journalist before the war. After her marriage, she recommenced the dreary but essential rounds of the provincial press, working in Kent and Nottinghamshire.

Anthony, whom everyone called 'Ant', found poorly paid jobs in engineering, mostly in the sales departments, and even with Carole working he never had enough money to own a racing car and enter it for track events.

Mr Harry Ashbrook, a Fleet Street man, who knew the Findlaters in Nottingham, described Carole as 'a power-house of ambition and energy while Ant seemed happy fiddling with carburettors'. It was Carole who decided that they had spent long enough in the provinces and without a definite job she came to London and got work as an Assistant Press Officer for the Royal Society for the Prevention of Accidents, ROSPA, a worthy body that has always had a tendency to employ ex-officers in key positions. 'Everyone', Carole remembers, 'stood up when the General came in in the morning.' This was clearly no place for a journalist.

Carole left ROSPA for a job at £20 a week as a subeditor on *Woman* magazine, which was more than Ant earned as a sales representative for a firm of neon sign manufacturers. This sense of financial inferiority, and the natural dulling of the early enthusiasms of marriage, produced an atmosphere where a triangle was almost a mathematical certainty. David Blakely was equipped by inclination and opportunity to form the third side.

Although Ant could not afford a racing car of his own, he was a devout fringe follower of the motor racing world; he and Carole had managed to buy an old Alfa-Romeo, which was their password to the mysterious freemasonry of racing drivers. It was this Alfa that David Blakely's friend had called to see at the Findlaters' flat, No. 52 Colet Gardens, Hammersmith. The deal was never made but two or three months later, David Blakely phoned Ant and told him that he had just bought an HRG sports car and would Ant care to come and have a look at it?

Ant was delighted and went round to Blakely's home at No 28 Culross Street, Mayfair, where David was living with Nanny and his brother Brian. David's mother and step-father were at No. 4 Culross Street. David might resent the smallness of his wage at the Hyde Park Hotel but certainly Mr Cook was providing an elegant home for him.

In the spring and early summer of 1951 David Blakely was an insistent caller at the Findlaters' flat. Carole was interested and flattered by the attention David showed. Ant was delighted with the business relationship he had established with David, for they had agreed to share the expense of racing the HRG. They competed as co-drivers in sports car races. Ant's responsibility was keeping the car running, for David Blakely was not really interested in what made the wheels move. His interest was in Carole.

To explain her late homecomings in the evenings Carole told Ant that she was attending meetings of the National Union of Journalists; an excuse used by many members of this highly respectable organization when they return home late or alcoholic. Instead of sitting on hard chairs in the upstairs, uncarpeted rooms of draughty pubs, the inevitable venue for NUJ branch sessions, Carole was meeting David in the 'Trevor Arms', a more comfortable pub in Knightsbridge, near the Hyde Park Hotel. Carole had many of the qualities David needed in women, as she was decisive, older than he, and captivated by his charm and good looks. She was not, however, the physical type that David usually preferred. Carole was dark and well-built, not blonde and frail-looking with thin ankles and wrists.

By the end of the summer, David was pleading with Carole to run away with him. He could not, as he unoriginally told her, live without her, he adored her, he needed her. Very few women, especially those whose marriages are in difficulties, and who have no children to anchor their emotions, can resist the old-fashioned combination of devotion and elopement. Carole decided to elope and went home to pack a bag. When she arrived at Colet Gardens, Ant was there. He watched her pack. It was Ant's turn now to declare that he could not live without her. Finally Carole's Jewish sense of home won, and she decided to stay with her husband. She telephoned David to tell him that she had changed her mind. A day or so later they met in the 'Trevor Arms', an edgy Carole and a disappointed David. Over half pints of bitter they discussed the situation.

David reassured Carole of his love, adding: 'I hope you didn't tell Ant who you were going to run off with?'

Carole said: 'Yes, I did, but it doesn't make any difference, does it?'

The romantic, the adoring, the handsome, the well-mannered Mr Blakely erupted with rage.

'You stupid bitch,' he shouted, 'now look what you've done. Who the bloody hell will tune my car now?'

That was understandably the end of any love Carole Find-later had for David Blakely, but despite his betrayal of his friend Ant, there was no break-up between the two men. The car, their god, bound them with an umbilical cord that convention could not cut.

It was not only motor cars that linked the two men, there were considerable emotional ties between them. To Ant David was a projection of himself, the boy who had always wanted to be a motor racing driver but who had been stopped by his father. Ant was determined that David should be a successful driver. To David, Ant was the bearded father figure who gave him all the encouragement that, rightly or wrongly, he felt was missing from his own family. On a more humdrum basis they were united in their dislike of regular and routine employment. When David was later working for Silicon Pistons, a small engineering firm at Penn, Bucks, he told his friend Cliff Davis, 'I can't stand work, it drives me potty.' David's ambition was to be a play-boy. To this end he cultivated the look of what he imagined to be the complete man about town, dark suit, rolled umbrella and bowler. He added to this would-be urbanity a rather schoolboy sense of fun. As one of his friends put it: 'David loved a good giggle.' This largely arose from David Blakely's wish to be popular, for basically he was lonely and insecure and giggling was a way to popularity, being one of the lads. Not everyone liked him, many of the racing car drivers though him pompous and stuck-up, because they did not realize that this was only lack of confidence. Some thought him mean at the bar, which was not true. When David had money he was extremely generous to his friends and he himself was a considerable drinker. During most of his friendship with the Findlaters he would often stand Ant's turn. When he was hard up David was too proud to admit it; it did not blend with the playboy image that he strove to create. He was a well-educated young man of the upper middle class with insufficient money to mix easily with his contemporaries. Of course he could have earned more money but that would have added the unpleasantness of hard work and leaving the not too exacting routine of a trainee at the Hyde Park Hotel, where there were plenty of women to pay for meals and drinks.

David's father died suddenly at his home in Sheffield on 24 February 1952, and David went North for the funeral. He was sixty-seven and had not remarried. He had died of a coronary thrombosis and there was a post-mortem but no inquest. David's two brothers were granted Letters of Administration and eventually the four Blakely children each received about £7,000 from their father's estate. As far as David was concerned it was a pity that Dr John had not followed that fine old British custom and left his money to a home for lost dogs or cats. The inheritance stimulated David to avoid work. Added to his inheritance, David also had the prospect of marrying money. One of the visitors to the Hyde Park Hotel was Miss Linda Dawson, the young, plump and expensively dressed daughter of a wealthy north country businessman. She was attracted by the handsome Mr Blakely and his dashing HRG sports car and David became a welcome guest at the Dawson home near Huddersfield, which, he proudly told his fellow-trainees, 'has a petrol pump in the grounds'. These visits to Miss Dawson, and her visits to him in London, accompanied by her family, did not stop David from sleeping with other women when she was out of town. He met his other girlfriends in drinking clubs in the Knightsbridge area. The most convenient for David was the Little Club in Brompton Road; by leaving from a side entrance to the hotel and ducking down the Underground subway outside the hotel that led to Knightsbridge station it was easy to emerge on the far side of the street and slip quietly into the Club.

Much of this visiting was done during the working hours and was covered up for him by friends on the staff at the hotel; occasionally they had to bother Mr Blakely on the phone to return to the hotel and help out.

David and his friends from the hotel liked the Little Club and there was a fair amount of undergraduate horseplay with the hostesses who worked there. This cooled off after one girl had a rib broken and threatened to sue. The hotel, of course, were not pleased with their trainee. Apart from the time off he wangled to go motor racing, and the sessions at the Little Club, Mr Blakely's heart was not in the business.

In October 1952, after a row with the banqueting manager, David was fired. His reaction was to appear at opening time the next morning in the hotel bar, where previously he had been forbidden to drink because he was on the staff, and order a large gin and tonic. Naturally he was dressed in his dark suit, with rolled umbrella and bowler hat.

Mrs Cook decided that perhaps travel might improve David's attitude to life; together they set off on a world cruise. David enjoyed it.

On his return to England, David told his friends that at one South American port he and another man had drunk their way around town. They were still drinking as the liner left port and they had to hire a launch, clambering aboard the ship by rope ladder. Recalling this incident, a friend of David's said: 'I'm sure this is true because when-ever David told you something awful that he'd done, he would go very white. This time his face was sheet-like.'

Back home David resumed doing the thing he did best: nothing. In the early part of 1953 he found a new diversion, an American model girl who was working in London. She was older than David, and married. It was a short affair and ended when the model returned to the United States.

David was still friends with the Findlaters and with his sister Maureen they made a foursome for pubbing and going to motor race meetings. Maureen, who was married to an American, usually stayed at 28 Culross Street when she came home on holiday and David was delighted that she and Ant Find-later got on so well.

When Mr and Mrs Cook moved from Culross Street to Penn in Bucks, one of those upper middle-class dormitories within easy motoring of London, David stayed at 28 Cul-ross Street. Later when he got a job with a Penn firm, Silicon Pistons, the Cooks gave him a flat in one wing of their new home. David's flat had a separate side entrance.

The new Cook home, 'The Old Park', was elegant and spacious and David's Nanny moved there from Culross Street. Despite this, and the pleasant privacy of his own flat, David spent little time there. He occasionally held parties for his motor-racing friends in the Penn flat but the bulk of his time was spent at Culross Street. A friend who went to a race meeting with David and the Cooks at this time recalls that it was not a very jolly outing. 'David and Humphrey sat over their beer just looking at each other, there was very lit-tle conversation between them. I got the impression that Humphrey was wondering what on earth he could do to make David realize that he must do something with his life.'

Whatever job he was doing at Silicon Pistons, and it varied from engineer to Works Manager, according to whom David was talking, it did not keep him away from the clubs and drink.

It was in a club that David had his second meeting with Ruth, who was now manageress of the Little Club, the first floor 3-11 pm drinking club of which David was already a member; he had joined when he worked at the Hyde Park Hotel. The club was owned by Morrie Conley and it had not been earning enough money to satisfy him.

The idea of making Ruth manageress followed her twenty-seventh birthday party that she had given at Carroll's Club, when Morrie had seen that Ruth had built up good connections, especially among the easy spending motor racing set.

The invitations to the party, printed on second-rate cards with scalloped edges, read: 'Ruth Ellis invites you to her Birthday Party on Friday, 9 October, at 7 pm. Cocktails and Buffet, 58 Duke Street, W1.' Ruth said that it cost £200 but never made it clear who paid. To her it was proof that she was someone of importance among the inhabitants of clubland.

What a soft-centred heap it was beneath the skin of sophistication and toughness of the hostesses and their regular boy friends. Have you ever wondered who buys those gut-turning birthday cards from the stationer? They are not the exclusive preserve of obscure, but respectable relatives, they obviously have a high sale among the worldly.

Ruth Ellis kept many of the cards sent to her on her twenty-seventh birthday. One consisted of pink roses and blue forget-me-nots on a lemon background with a Cambridge blue bow at the side. Another card featured an old-fashioned thatched cottage in a silver-paper oval frame. The frame was decorated by bunches of blue daisies and pink dog roses, while in the right-hand side was a vast golden bowl, made from metal foil from which sprouted vast red roses.

Inside was the artist's conception of the Olde Englishe country garden, complete with lily pond, fountain and hollyhocks. The verse read:

> 'A simple birthday greeting,
> But because it comes to you,
> The thoughts and wishes it conveys
> Are specially warm and true;
> May all the joys that make life sweet
> By Yours this happy day,
> The dreams you treasure in your heart
> Come true in every way.'

One dream certainly came true. For years Ruth had wanted a club of her own and this was the proposition that Morrie Conley, that astute businessman, was now to offer her.

The terms were reasonable and businesslike. Ruth was to get a basic salary of £15 a week and a £10 a week entertainment allowance. There was a two-roomed flat, with a kitchen, over the club which was to be rent-free. Later there were two other inhabitants of two separate rooms over the club, both girls, and Ruth was to share the bathroom with them. These girls were not among the three hostesses that Morrie promised Ruth she could have to help with the club.

Ruth was enchanted with the deal. To her it was the summit to be the boss of a smart club in a 'good' neighbourhood—to be someone important. It did not deter her that the two rooms above the club, like many of the flats at Gilbert Court where she had been living, were tenanted by Morrie's call-girls; after all she was one herself, except that she preferred 'steady' protectors.

This was the reality about which the majority of the club's members knew nothing. The girls in the rooms upstairs did not use the club for soliciting; the business was discreet.

The club membership was predominantly middle class, businessmen, RAF officers, alcoholics with private incomes, and the flotsam fringe of dishonesty that moves like a muck-strewn tide between Chelsea, Belgravia, and Knightsbridge. Adding a little dirty froth at the edges of the stream were the confidence men and professional criminals who use clubs; the former for suckers, the latter to spend their loot among people who ask no questions.

Ruth had cards printed to advertise the club. The card itself was a pastel shade of blue, the lettering maroon, and on the left-hand side of the card was a golden knight on horseback, his lance pointing to the ground. The card was as tasteless as the club decor, with its coy wall mirrors from which electric candelabra projected. The electric bulbs were topped with pleated shades edged at the top and bottom with gold braid.

Ruth later recalled that David Blakely was the first customer she ever served at the Little Club and that he looked surprised and nervous when he recognized that the blonde at the bar was the girl with whom he had brushed a few weeks ago at Carroll's.

Naturally, Ruth Ellis was not rude, as she had learned as a club hostess that losing your temper with customers is financially disastrous. Her ambition 'to make something of her life' also publicly damped down her tremendous temper and for years she had built her public image of a cool, equable, good-natured woman, who took life as it happened.

There were no scenes with Blakely's first gin and tonic at the Little Club under the new management, and Ruth Ellis recalled that there was *very* little enthusiasm on his part either. She said that David was 'playing hard to get' and 'I suppose that was part of his attraction'.

Doubtless some of this hard-to-get quality was the reaction to his recent engagement to Miss Linda Dawson, the girl David had met when he was working at the Hyde Park Hotel and whose dowry might reasonably be expected to include the promise that one day David would inherit that coveted petrol pump in the grounds. It was a match approved by Mrs Cook and the official announcement appeared in *The Times* on 11 November 1953.

A playboy needs playgirls even if engaged and after their re-introduction David saw that Ruth would provide what every playboy needs, the undemanding bed-ability of a girl looking for kicks with a man outside her social class but upon whom she would make no demands of stability, respectability or matrimony. At first all went according to plan. After two weeks, David, a constant heavy spender at the bar, had persuaded Ruth to allow him to sleep with her in the flat over the Club. He had to adapt to Ruth's other arrangements for her customers upstairs, but she was reasonably available to David. Ruth and the other hostesses at the Club at this time referred to him as 'Loverboy' and apart from paying for food and drink there was no question of David paying for sleeping with Ruth. She could attend to business in the afternoons. David was her night choice.

At her trial at the Old Bailey, Ruth Ellis gave her Counsel, Mr Melford Stevenson, QC, an honest and dispassionate account of the early days of their affair.

Q. Did he come and live with you in a flat which you occupied above the club?
A. Yes.

Q. At that time how did he behave towards you?

A. He was very concerned about me. He seemed very devoted.

Q. At that time you were still married?

A. Yes [to George Ellis].

Q. And was he engaged to another young woman?

A. Yes.

Q. Did he come to sleep at your flat nearly every night, and did he spend the weekends at Penn [Mr Cook's home]?

A. He stayed there from Monday to Friday, and spent the weekends in Penn.

Q. And at that time were you very much in love with him?

A. Not really.

Q. As time went on, how did he show his feelings for you?

A. In the December of that year [1953] I had an abortion by him and he was very concerned about my welfare. Although he was engaged to another girl, he offered to marry me, and he said it seemed unnecessary for me to get rid of the child, but I did not want to take advantage of him.

Q. When he offered to marry you, what did you say to that? How did you take it?

A. I was not really in love with him at the time, and it was quite unnecessary to marry me. I thought I could get out of the mess quite easily.

Q. What mess?

A. I decided I could get out of the mess quite easily.

The Judge, Mr Justice Havers. You mean the child?

A. Yes.

Q. Without him marrying you?

A. Yes.

Mr Stevenson: Did you in fact get out of the trouble in the
    way you have described in February 1954?
A. That is quite correct.
Mr Justice Havers: You had an abortion?
A. Yes.

As both Ruth and David can no longer answer questions
the truth about this incident is guesswork. Plainly Ruth was
not clear about the date of the abortion, saying first it was
in December and then in February. The latter is almost
certainly the right date, unless she had two in that period.
As Blakely did not sleep with her until late October at the
earliest, but more likely mid-November, a December abortion was unlikely.

The pregnancy that was terminated in February may not
have been the result of her association with Blakely, but
could have been caused by another of her clients. There was
no need for her to have mentioned the abortion in Court, a
move not calculated to win much sympathy from the jury,
if she did not believe that Blakely was the father. Feminine
intuition about conception dates is often right.

The abortion took place one weekend when David was
out of town. Blakely knew it was arranged and while he
was away telephoned often to see whether Ruth was all
right. When she recalled the incident later she wrote: 'I
did not ask him for, and he did not pay or offer, any money
for the operation, although at that time he certainly had
some.'

Whether Blakely really offered to marry her at this time
is doubtful. In any case he was safe in making the offer as
Ruth obviously made it clear to him that the club came
before children. If he did propose it was probably the

proposal that many men have made in moments of alcoholic compassion and rejected in sober realism.

Whatever David may have told Ruth in private about being prepared to marry her, he was certainly not echoing it in public; as far as his friends were aware he was still going to marry Miss Dawson.

For some months after the abortion Ruth and David still regarded each other as desirable conveniences; to her it was flattering to have this educated, very personable man lusting for her. To him Ruth was something to boast about to the boys and a woman who, being indifferent about sex, was unworried by his inadequate sexual technique. He found her long-practised bedroom acrobatics irresistible, and he bragged of them to Ant Findlater. There was one incident that he did not discover about his mistress's private life.

Occasionally Ruth would take a night off from David and the Little Club and visit her old girlfriends who were still working as hostesses at West End clubs. On one of these jaunts she and another hostess were invited back to the home of a Kensington businessman to continue drinking after the club shut. Although she was both a heavy drinker and smoker at this time, and she had the true drinker's habit of only eating one small meal a day, Ruth was not the excessive compulsive drinker that she became just before she shot Blakely. The morning after the 'party' the two women went home and the businessman discovered that a substantial sum of money was missing. The police were called and advised the man to be quite sure before he made a specific charge against either or both the women. The police then had a 'friendly' chat with Ruth; the money was returned. Whether the money was stolen or the man, in drink, had paid it for services from the two girls is unknown.

David Blakely too was doing silly things when drunk. The money left by his father enabled him to buy much more gin than he could hold and unpleasantness, like the incident when Cliff Davis had to rescue him from an irate Mike Hawthorn after David put ice down his back, became more common.

The playboy image was beginning to look blurred to many of the younger members of the clubs used by David Blakely. The alcohol did not dispel David's doubts, the loneliness and the longing to belong. Unfortunately the money made it more difficult for him to be accepted as 'one of the lads'. David would enter a bar and order, say fifteen double gins for his set, and very few for whom he bought drinks had the wish, or the money, to join a school like that. Soon it was understood that to mix with Blakely could embarrass you into buying drinks for people you did not know, or want to know.

Consequently David spent more and more time at the Little Club where Ruth was always pleased to see him, and he was tolerated by other members even when drunk and objectionable, because he was a boyfriend of Ruth's. Ruth overlooked his outbursts, because not only was David spending a lot of money in her bar, but he was encouraging those who still wanted his friendship to come to the Little Club. He was proud to ask them along to meet Ruth, whom he described to them as 'a smashing blonde'. He still had friends but they were nearly all older men, like Lionel Leonard and Cliff Davis, racing car drivers who appreciated David's skill on the track and hoped that in a few years a lot of the youthful nonsense would disappear. They saw that he had a potential for good, and they were right. The trouble was that David had little will for developing it; as long as he was hanging around the Little Club bar in a half-drunken haze, David would certainly never exert what small amount of will-power he had.

After considerable nagging from Ruth, David took her to motor race meetings where she could be seen by the other 'boys'; it was a considerable boost to the ego of what her husband, George Ellis, had called 'that bloody bitch from Brixton' to be mixing with men and women who on the surface were 'good class'. The first time David took her racing with him she wore a sheath dress, but she learned quickly and bought the necessary tweeds, scarves, and sensible footwear that were the uniform at these events.

To please David she often went with him to the cinema, a form of entertainment which bored her and which he adored. In return he accompanied Ruth to the theatre which she liked and David detested. Usually their evenings out consisted of heavy pub-crawling and visits to clubs where Ruth's friends worked as hostesses or were members. She was eager to show them what a well-bred young man she had in tow; David too was flattered to introduce the smart, brassy, and apparently sophisticated Ruth to his friends, for she was a mistress to be envied by less fortunate young men. He even introduced her to Mrs Findlater, she had already met Ant at the Little Club. Mrs Findlater's first meeting with Ruth was on Ant's birthday in April 1954.

David told Carole that he would have to leave the party early as he had promised to take Ruth out. Carole, who had heard some time before from her husband that David had started a new affair, telephoned Ruth at the Little Club and asked her to come over. The invitation was a mixture of politeness and curiosity; Carole wanted to inspect David's new mistress. Mrs Findlater can recall exactly her first meeting with Ruth: 'She was wearing a black dress with a plunging neckline; she had a small bust, small wrists and ankles, the effect was shrimplike. She said "Hello" to me in a tiny voice when we were introduced, and then ignored me for the rest of the evening. She spent all her time talking to every man at the party. I was not impressed but I was determined to be polite for Ant and David's sake.'

Ruth Ellis too remembered this meeting. 'Carole behaved like the Mother Superior herself, but I took no notice as I didn't want any unpleasantness for David's sake.'

Despite the outings and the parties Ruth began to find 'loverboy' a problem. First he upset the staff by his callow behaviour, squirting soda water at friends and acquaintances. This so annoyed Mrs Jackie Dyer, the barmaid, that she took a syphon and gave Mr Blakely a cooling shower. Like a boy who has been hit by another lad at school, David left the bar and ran upstairs to Ruth in her flat; he demanded that Mrs Dyer should be sacked. Naturally Ruth was not going to risk a staff rumpus over a silly incident. This is how she analysed the situation: 'I began to think that it was time that the affair [with Blakely] ended, because we seemed to be getting too deeply involved, the business at the club was beginning to suffer because of my now frequent absences and the fact that I was being monopolized. Furthermore, the proprietor of the club had started charging me a rental for the flat because he knew that David was living there and he had already warned me that he objected to it. He considered that it was bad for me and the business.'

There was also jealousy in Morrie Conley's action; it was accepted at his clubs that Morrie was still very attracted to Ruth.

# 5

# Ruth's Alternative Lover

Ruth decided that someone should replace 'loverboy' as a drinking companion and escort, but she did not want to lose David altogether. The compromise she chose was unoriginal but as always, workable; she began to flirt with one of David's friends. Mr Desmond Cussen had met Ruth when she was at Carroll's and had been brought to the Little Club by David.

Desmond Cussen was then thirty-three and was a director in the family business of Cussen & Co, wholesale and retail tobacconists, with their main depot at No. 93 Peckham High Street, SE 15, where he had his office. He was a bachelor and lived in a self-contained flat, No. 20 Goodwood Court, Devonshire Street, W I, just off Harley Street.

During the war he had served with the RAF but in appearance he was quite unlike the conventional wartime RAF man; his dark brown hair was oiled back smoothly and he had a thin moustache, which gave him, with his small, square figure and round face, a faintly oriental look. He was not particularly outstanding in anything he did, except the extremely competent way he drove his black Ford Zodiac; he was a man on the fringe of the racing car driving clique.

He was also very much in love with Ruth Ellis. A shy man, very much in awe of his mother, Desmond Cussen was proud to be seen escorting a woman like Ruth who seemed to him so assured and sophisticated. He described her to me as 'sexually very mechanical, but great fun to be at a party with'. Ruth used his infatuation to encourage him to spend as much time and money as possible at the bar. Some nights she would devote herself to Desmond and ignore David, on others she would reverse the treatment. It increased the jealousy of both without reducing their ardour. David however had the clinching reassurance that in the early days it was he who slept with Ruth not Desmond. The triangular game of love did not please the unpleasant Mr Conley.

A former member of the Little Club recalled a visit Morrie paid there at this time: 'He came into the bar unexpectedly. David was sitting at one end of the bar while Ruth was laughing and talking with Desmond at the other. When Morrie came to the counter everyone stopped talking, the silence was quite awful. It was like some scene from a Hollywood gangster film.'

The competition between David Blakely and Desmond Cussen for Ruth's complete attention decided David that he would out-glamorize his rival; not only would he be the promising young racing car driver but he would also own a racing sports car built to his conception. He knew that the excitement and prestige of this move would appeal to Ruth's lust for 'getting on' socially and he hoped that, happy in his reflected power, Ruth would forget the solid, unexciting devotion of the tobacco salesman.

Despite the double gins and the overheads of the playboy image, David still had some money left from his inheritance. The obvious partner in this plan to build a 'special' was that ever-eager racing car buff, Ant Findlater. Ant's early training and his current job with Aston-Martin, the racing and sports car experts, ensured that he had the technical know-how to construct a special. There was one immediate obstacle to this plan; by the time it was discussed and agreed, Mrs Findlater was eight months pregnant and had given up her £20 a week magazine job. If Ant left Aston-Martin how would they live in reasonable comfort? David offered Ant £10 a week to work for him on the new project. It meant that Carole would have to manage on a shoestring, so her agreement was vital. She said that Ant must do what he thought best; Ant immediately handed in his notice at Aston-Martin. There were dangers in the situation. If the new project ran out of money, or happy-go-lucky David forgot to pay Ant for a week or two, Carole quite understandably was going to resent her decision.

At first, of course, all was for the best in the euphoria of the new idea. David rented a former china warehouse in Islington as a workshop for the car. Here for the next six months, Ant worked up to eighteen hours a day on the special. The body was bought as a complete unit for £375 and the engine, the latest 1,500 cc Singer-HRG was supplied to them on very favourable terms.

Ant and David had co-driven a conventional HRG for three seasons and the firm had confidence in them. Apart from the engine and body, the car, which was named the 'Emperor' was a hotch-potch of other people's components and some very skilled 'home-made' improvisations by Ant. The Emperor was not only conceived as a race winner, but as the prototype of a specialist sports car that would sell to enthusiasts at about £1,000. The project was heavily under-capitalized, therefore certain to fail.

The spring of 1954 was important for most of the

characters in this story. George Ellis, Ruth's husband, had reappeared and was a steady customer at the Little Club when he came to town from his home in Walton, Warrington in Lancashire. Here, despite his heavy drinking, he was employed as a schools' dental officer; child lovers should remember that this job was then one of the worst paid sectors of dentistry, and the authorities could not be too fussy about the men they employed.

Despite their matrimonial differences, George and Ruth jogged on. Occasionally, she allowed him to sleep on a divan in the sitting room when he was too drunk to go home. One of the reasons for George's visits was Georgina, the baby of the marriage who was living with Ruth in the flat together with the boy Andria. It was agreed that it would be best for the girl if she went North with George and was later adopted. This, fortunately, happened. George also wanted to discuss his forthcoming petition for divorce on the grounds of cruelty which was lodged in the High Court on 26 May, 1954. Ruth was determined to defend the action to keep her allowance of £4 a week from her husband.

In May 1954 Mrs Findlater had a daughter, Francesca, and David was to be one of her god-parents. The birth of Francesca put more strain on the Findlater budget, and apart from the financial issue, an emotional problem was added to the family's difficulties. David and Ant were riveted to the building of the Emperor and Carole saw very little of her husband when she felt she needed him most. There were rows about the time he spent with David, and their drinking in the Little Club after work; Carole's attitude to David became more hostile and critical. However, the bond of the car between the two men was far too tough to be affected by Carole's reaction.

Ruth continued to let David spend nights at the Little Club but after Morrie's warning over the rent she was more careful about the business. She gave more of her Sunday afternoon parties to which she invited anyone who would come, provided they had money or some show business cachet. The parties did increase the club membership and the guests were fodder for name-droppers at the club. You got bit actors instead of salted peanuts.

One of the guests was the film actor Richard Greene, who was not yet delighting the young of all ages in most countries with his with-one-bound-he-was-free performance in the TV series 'Robin Hood'.

David was jealous of Ruth's flattery of her men customers and the obvious devotion of Desmond Cussen and he accused her of 'tarting around the bar'. Ruth was unaffected by David's jealousy. To her it was proper that she should be the pursued and it was revenge for the 'hard-to-get' approach by David that so stung her at the beginning of their affair.

Ruth and Desmond ignored David's jealousy and went to race meetings together and did the usual circuit of the clubs. Cussen was very much in love with Ruth and would certainly have married her if she had pleased.

Ruth herself was not willing to marry anyone at this time. She was not free to do so but it was more vital to her to become a person of importance in the club world. Her analysis of the situation was that she could use Cussen as a foil to 'loverboy' who eventually would get married to Linda Dawson and that would be that.

Occasionally there were rows between Ruth and David. During one Ruth told him that it was stupid to worry about her as he spent most evenings in the bar and later in the flat.

To which David said: 'It's not what you do at nights that worries me – it's what you do in the afternoons.' It is unlikely that this was more than a guess, at this stage of their relationship, of the way in which Ruth made more money.

It is improbable that Blakely would have given her money for sex; there were plenty of women who would provide that for nothing and in turn she could afford the pleasure of a genuine lover. His good looks and social position were sufficient compensation. At this time too it seems certain that Ruth was not sleeping with Desmond Cussen, although she was borrowing money from him. On one occasion she told Cussen that she could not understand why he should lend her money without wanting something in return. The answer was elementary: Cussen was in love. Ruth had told Cussen all the details of her past, except the true story of Andria's father, but he did know that the child was illegitimate. George Ellis was portrayed to Desmond as a drunken bully but the background of Ruth's obsessive nagging and jealousy was omitted.

The retelling of how hard life had been was part of her act with men. A former lover of Ruth's, looking back ten years later, summed it up: 'She told me all her troubles but then I thought I was the only one who knew. It wasn't until years after that I discovered that she pitched this tale to all of us.

'She used to tell the most awful lies to get money from you, in the end I used to say "Look, here's a couple of quid". It was the only way to get rid of her she was so damn persistent.'

At this stage, Desmond's money went on clothes and paying the rent which Morrie wanted for the flat. David still had some of his father's inheritance in the bank and she was not giving Desmond's money to him.

In early June 1954, David Blakely went to Le Mans as a co-driver in the 24-hour race and on 11 June he sent a post-card to Ruth from Le Mans of the monument to the fallen in the 1914-18 war, an admirable, if unromantic, choice.

On the postcard, he wrote in his feminine, immature scrawl, 'Arrived O.K. Haven't had a drink for three days!!! Wish you were here, will see you Tuesday. Love, David.' It was sent to the Little Club. Tuesday came but David did not return. If he wrote to explain why he was delayed, the letter no longer exists, which is strange for Ruth Ellis was squirrel-like about paper and kept the most trivial scribble. What probably happened was that David had the chance to drive at other meetings abroad and decided to stay. It was a deci-sion that stung the possessive Mrs Ellis.

This was Desmond Cussen's moment of opportunity. The trouble was that he found it difficult to make an open proposal of sexual intercourse. Some women find this shy-ness charming, most find it unflattering. To Ruth, who was very practical and businesslike about sex, it was just stupid, especially as Desmond had loaned her money without ask-ing for anything in exchange. According to Desmond it was Ruth who gave the invitation for him to sleep with her at the Little Club flat. There was, on Ruth's part, no question of love between them. Ruth herself was drinking very heavily at the time and the affair may have been launched by her in a mood of alcoholic abandon.

Infatuated and sex-dozened, as he afterwards admitted, Desmond would have married Ruth but she was indiffer-ent. The motive of the affair was to reassure herself that if 'lover-boy' stayed away there were men to replace him immediately. A secondary motive was that she was still worried about Morrie Conley's clear dislike of the affair with David. Already he had made her pay rent, the next move could be to appoint a new manageress. After all the effort it was not worth risking the Little Club for 'loverboy'.

On 2 July, David sent Ruth another postcard, this time from Rheims; it was a picture of the Fontaine Subé in the Place Drouet d'Erlon. David Blakely obviously had a taste for these phallic piles of French provincial architecture. He wrote: 'Darling, have arrived safely and am having quite a good time. The cars are going very well. Looking forward to seeing you. David. P.S. Love to Desmond!!!' He had a penchant for exclamation marks.

Whether the reference to Desmond was guesswork or whether he had heard from Ruth that she was going out with him is unknown. More likely it was a piece of natural jealousy. As soon as David arrived back in England a few days later, he went to the Little Club. Ruth had missed him, for he was a more witty and entertaining companion that the devoted Desmond, whose idea of humour was to say 'Yais' to almost any remark. He also had the decisive advantage of looking more 'county' than Desmond to the class-constipated Mrs Ellis.

Ruth's explanation for the affair with Cussen and what happened after David returned was given at the Old Bailey in answers to questions from her leading Counsel, Mr Melford Stevenson.

Q. When you had that affair with Cussen, what did you hope or think might happen as far as Blakely and you were concerned?

A. I thought it might finish it; I thought that Desmond would tell David we had been intimate, and I thought that would finish it.

Neither Desmond nor Ruth did in fact tell David and Mr Stevenson then asked:

Q. But what happened as far as you and Blakely were concerned?

A. At that time he was getting – David was getting – rather jealous. He asked me what I had been doing, and all kinds of things like that, and, of course, I did not tell him.

Q. Did your association with Blakely in fact end there?

A. It began again.

Q. At whose insistence. His or yours?

A. David's.

Q. Did you try to avoid that happening?

A. It was very difficult. I was running a business, and he was there all the time. He was entitled to walk in; he was a customer, and he was hanging around the bar all the time. He was spending money in my bar. I could not tell him to go away.

While David was in Le Mans, and before, Ruth had been telling Desmond that she wanted to break with David. Even if this were true, and it was probably one of Ruth's lies to encourage Desmond to lend her money, the situation between Ruth and David had returned to normal. To her it was one of businesslike pleasure; to David it was still one of sexual infatuation geared to a high tension and fed by drink and jealousy. Ruth's independence irked him. He had tried protestations of love but she was still the dominant partner.

All his life, from his old nanny to the married women who adored him, David had been a spoiled boy with women; they had always surrendered completely to him. In the sex war with Ruth Ellis, there was still one weapon left which might defeat her, a proposal of marriage.

Soon after David's return from France Ruth decided that she would throw a belated birthday party for him, as he had been abroad on 17 June, his twenty-fifth birthday. To this party Ruth invited many of the Club 'regulars', those of David's motor racing friends who were still on drinking terms with him, and the Findlaters. Neither Carole nor Ruth liked each other and the party only made the relationship worse. By some conscious or subconscious motivation, Ruth squirted Carole with a soda syphon, and in the excitement Carole laddered her nylons. It was the kind of semi-drunken horseplay that either gets the big laugh or the deep freeze. Mrs Findlater left the club for Hampstead in a huff. It was a small 'incident' in the war between these two women. After Francesca was born a sober and very subdued Ruth went to tea at No. 29 Tanza Road with a present for the baby. It was a thirty guinea christening robe. Mrs Findlater never took it out of the box and some years later gave it to Boy Scouts who were collecting for a jumble sale. She did not tell them the origin of the robe but warned them 'not to sell it for nothing as it was very valuable'.

David too had not been the perfect guest, arriving very late, around eleven, moody and curt. By the early hours those who remained had assumed the tolerance of professional drinkers and were amiable if not coherent. By these standards the party was a success, and as they were the only standards that Ruth Ellis knew about parties, she looked back on it with satisfaction.

Subsequently David told Ruth why he had been late for the party. He had been across the road, in the bar of the Hyde Park Hotel with his fiancée, Linda Dawson, and the engagement had been broken off. Who decided to end it is unknown; David told Ruth the decision was his, if so, why did he not tell her immediately he arrived at the club, and why was he so morose that evening? It is more likely that Miss Dawson was tired of being neglected or that she had heard about the affair with Ruth. Whatever the reason, it was a decision that was to allow David to attack Ruth's emotional impregnability unhindered.

Ruth's account of the breaking of the engagement is this: 'I was in the flat with him one night and I asked him when he was getting married and he said: "I've got news for you, you are not going to lose me after all. I've broken my engagement." I said I thought that he had been callous and heartless and asked him if he had not any feelings for her to which he replied "None whatever".

'From then on he paid even more attention to me, he literally adored me, my hands, my eyes, everything except my peroxided hair, which he always wanted to be brunette.

'Now he was free, I am afraid I allowed myself to become very attached to him. At that time I thought the world of him; I put him on the highest of pedestals. He could do nothing wrong and I trusted him implicitly.'

The cause of this deepening in her relationship with David Blakely was that once more he had asked her to marry him. The proposal was reinforced by displays of excessive jealousy on his part. It was a flattering reversal of the terms on which the relationship had begun; then David had played hard to get, now it was her turn.

It must have seemed to Ruth that life was treating her

well. She was a success both in business and romance, although in her practical way she was still not wholly sure that the situation was as good as it seemed. Her analysis was this: 'I still, however, did not think seriously of the possibility of marriage.

I myself was still married and I believed from what he had told me about his family that his mother would never allow such a marriage.'

Rejected by Linda Dawson, David made an impulsive offer to Ruth which flattered her but which had no immediate impact on her plans.

Neither David nor Ruth allowed the prospect of marriage however distant, to curb their separate sex lives. As Desmond admitted at Hampstead Magistrates Court later, the affair between him and Ruth did not end on David's return from France. Ruth also continued her call-girl activities. David too compensated for Desmond with his other 'steady' mistress, a talkative blonde who worked as an usherette at a West End theatre and who treated David impeccably. She was older, as one would expect, than David and to her he was a spoiled boy to be pitied and mothered, but never a man to be deeply loved.

One of David's dalliances with her was discovered by Ruth who was correspondingly petulant. Ruth described the incident later, certainly with more control than she greeted it at the time.

'One night he got into bed and was stretching over to switch out the light when I noticed love bites all over his shoulders, back and neck. I went quite cold with shock and I told him to get out and leave the flat. He said he could explain everything and started to tell me that someone had bitten him in the neck while he was playing darts at Penn.

I said "Please get out of my bed and out of my flat, and don't come near me again".'

At the Old Bailey she told Mr Melford Stevenson what happened then.

Q. Was there a row about it?

A. No, I just asked him to go. He did not like it, but he went.

Q. How long did he remain away?

A. He 'phoned about an hour after he had left the premises, and he 'phoned early in the morning and told me he had spent the night at Islington [presumably in the garage workshop there], and he was very cold and miserable and asked if he could come back, and I said 'No'. He returned as soon as the bar opened up at three o'clock, and went into my bar, and asked my barmaid if he could see me, and I had already instructed the barmaid that I was not at home to him. He 'phoned then from the box just in the entrance to the club to my place upstairs, and asked if he could please come up, and I said 'No'.

After half-an-hour he came upstairs, and I was fooling around in the flat, doing one thing and another. He was very emotionally upset, and he went on his knees crying and saying: 'I'm sorry, darling. I do love you. I'll prove it,' and he asked me to marry him and I said: 'I don't think your mother or family will agree to this.'

Q. What did he say about that?

A. He said that if there was any trouble with his family we could get married secretly.

Q. Is it right to say that at this time the proceedings for the dissolution of your marriage were going on?

A. Yes.

Q. How did they terminate? First of all, was it a defended divorce case?

A. No, I did not defend myself.

Q. Not in the end, but had it been defended up to that time?

A. Yes, yes.

Q. Why did it cease to be defended?

A. Because I wanted a divorce, and I decided not to claim any maintenance or defend myself in any way and also give up my husband and daughter.

Q. Did the divorce go through?

A. Yes, undefended.

Q. You say you did that on the ground that you were going to marry David? Is that right?

A. Yes.

Two points are clear from this court episode. First the great pride that Ruth had in being the manageress of the Little Club; this emerges in the references to 'my bar' and 'my barmaid'. Then there is the proof that after the 'love bite' incident and Blakely's renewed offer of marriage, Ruth had decided that she would now take the offer seriously, even if it had to be fulfilled in secret. The story she told that she had given up Georgina for the sake of David was not true; the child's future adoption had been decided between George Ellis and his wife several months previously.

Although Ruth was prepared to admit that David's family would never agree to the marriage she was shrewd enough to realize that much of this opposition would end if they married in secret and the family was presented with the *fait accompli*. By now her lust for security had been reinforced by clandestine all night visits to David's flat at Penn and the realization that the Cook family lived in considerable style and luxury.

It is a pity that when George Ellis and David Blakely met, as they did occasionally in the Little Club, that the two men could not have discussed Ruth and her reactions as a married woman. George, if he had been sober enough, could have told David that matrimony or its immediate prospect turned Ruth from a woman with whom it was tolerably easy to live with into a shrew. David, like many men, had succeeded in talking himself lightly into a situation from which he calculated his charm would safely extricate him. If the engagement grew too fraught he could always end it with a few civilized gin and tonics at the Hyde Park Hotel.

This kind of game requires a civilized opponent like Miss Linda Dawson. Ruth was untrained in this middle-class game of love.

What did Ruth Ellis mean by love? She appeared to her friends, and in particular to Mrs Dyer who served at the Little Club bar, to be 'in love' with David. Certainly she was clinging, jealous, possessive, and anxious to care for him. In Holloway, she told a visiting cleric: 'If he had cut his finger I would have gone to the ends of the earth to bandage it.' First-aid is not an unquestioned proof of love. All that can be said now is that at the time Ruth Ellis believed that she was in love with David Blakely.

In August 1954 David went to the International Sports Car meeting at Zandvoort in Holland to race an MG car owned by his friend Lionel Leonard, a well-to-do motor racing enthusiast who had several other MGS built to his own specification. The conventional good time was had by all but David unluckily did little racing. His picture appeared in the magazine *Autosport* with the caption 'wow! David

Blakely hastily straps down the Leonard–MG's bonnet after viewing the horrible mess caused by throwing a con rod.'

David had asked Ruth to come with him but she could not leave the club. August is never a good month for drinking clubs; even their members have to surrender to the women and children sometimes and go on holiday. Conscious that Morrie Conley was watching the takings Ruth decided that it would pay her better to stay and persuade what customers there were to buy as many drinks as possible. To Ruth the Little Club was 'her' club and still the most important thing in her life.

The first dangerous crisis in the Ellis–Blakely love affair was in the autumn of 1954. It arose, like so many crises between the sexes, over money. David's inheritance had almost gone, gobbled away by building the Emperor at Islington, getting drunk with Ruth, and the overheads of race meetings. He still had his allowance and his wages from Silicon Pistons but this could not support the playboy image and pay for the occasional entertainment of ladies with enjoyable back-biting habits. The £10 a week that he was supposed to pay Ant Find-later was often owing and Carole Findlater decided that she must work again. She did not want to be separated from baby Francesca but it was inescapable. This was a situation that did not make David Blakely a very welcome visitor to Tanza Road. The coolness was temporarily eased when Carole was commissioned by a women's magazine to go to Russia to write a series for £500.

Ruth too was having money problems. Her son Andy would be ten in September and there was the question of his schooling. The boy himself wanted to be a scientist, for he had all his mother's urge for self-improvement.

Ruth decided that he should go to a boarding prep

school, a move which had two advantages. She thought that it would give the boy a better 'start in life', and it would get him out of the crowded flat for a considerable part of the year. By now Andy was a world-wise Londoner. He accepted the men in his mother's bed-life as 'Uncles' and he had been very happy down at Warsash with George Ellis. Like his mother he had been proud that George was a 'dental surgeon' and therefore much 'better class' than the people he had met when living with Granny at Brixton. Ruth loved him in the same way as she loved David – selfishly. She was prepared to do anything for him that did not mean giving up what she wanted to do. He was shuttled between her various homes and her mother's house at Ruth's whim. So the boy had plenty of pocket money, late hours, little discipline from Ruth (because that would have meant taking trouble with him) and an appetite for those foods like steak and frozen peas which can be prepared easily and quickly. Andy knew all the museums in the South Kensington area backwards and all the attendants knew him. The London Underground, that haven for bored and neglected children, was his playground as he devised long, complicated journeys on those lines that go to improbable places like Deb-den. When Andy was about six he had been knocked down by a motor car and hurt his head. Possibly as a result he was a clumsy child about the house and was always breaking things accidentally.

The financial difficulty over sending Andy to boarding school was solved by the obliging Mr Cussen who, although he knew that Ruth was sleeping with David, had not been discouraged. In August 1954 he took Ruth by car to see a prospective headmaster and when she had decided to send Andy there he helped her buy the school uniform, drove them to the school at the beginning of the term and later went down and paid the fees.

This removed the most immediate money worry but it did not solve the cash problem which David Blakely soon became for her. He told Ruth that he was broke and all his earnings would now have to be spent on the Emperor. He reinforced his story of poverty by arriving very upset late one night at the Club. Ruth asked him what the trouble was, and David explained he had just had a row with his stepfather who had threatened to cut his allowance because he was spending too much time in the 'Crown' at Penn. Like a spoiled child, David's first reaction was to run away from home and he asked Ruth if he could move into her flat. She did not want David to know about her call-girl activities, and she said no. David's reaction was predictable. He threatened suicide if he were rejected. Ruth told him not to be so silly and David stayed on in his flat at Penn. In fact he did what 'Mummy' said.

Ruth was anxious for the car to be finished; it would make David happy and be a status symbol for her when they went to race meetings. Ruth eased his money troubles for him by allowing him to drink and buy cigarettes on credit at the Little Club. The considerable number of drinks he bought for others also went 'on the slate'. Ruth gave him free meals in the small club restaurant, especially at week-ends. In addition, she would often pay for their evenings out. She either handed him the cash, or, if he wrote a cheque, would give him the money to cover it. It was not a tolerable position for David Blakely as a man. Ruth's realistic friends described it as 'poncing'.

David could rationalize it as temporary dependence on Ruth until the Emperor was ready and had been successfully raced. After that there would be plenty of money from selling production models at £1,000 each. The completion of the Emperor was delayed not only by money shortages but by Ant Findlater's need to earn money, urged on by Carole who had returned from Russia. By day he existed as a secondhand motor car salesman; at night he worked on the car which had been transferred from Islington to the large garage at 28 Culross Street, in order to economize. It would have helped if David had worked consistently on the car in the evenings. Unfortunately now that drink was on the house at the Little Club he was drunk most evenings. This in turn meant that when he left for Penn in the mornings he had a hangover, so he was often in 'The Crown' at Penn at opening time for a 'livener'. By closing time after lunch David would be alcoholically topped up again and the few quick ones after work in the evenings at 'The Crown' before he left for the Little Club would ensure that he frequently arrived there drunk.

Ruth was worried because there was a limit to the drink that David could have without her paying for it eventually.

Morrie Conley did not allow the staff to pocket more than what he regarded as reasonable 'perks'. Ruth had an entertainment allowance of £10 a week but that did not pay for David's drinking and smoking as well as buying the customers a round on the house. Her wages and commission on drink sales a week had always been supplemented by her call-girl activities. Now Morrie had started charging £10 a week rent and David had become so jealous and suspicious that it meant that her income was reduced. There remained the club petty cash but this had to be put back eventually; Morrie was a careful book-keeper.

Her own drinking was principally paid for by the

customers and she would start on gin and tonic or gin and ginger ale as soon as the bar opened at 3 pm and continue until the bar closed officially at 11 pm. After hours there would be more drinking, either at impromptu parties in the flat upstairs or with David in the bar, or in the flat alone. Originally a bottle of Pernod had been stocked so that customers could offer Jackie Dyer, the French-born barmaid, a drink she liked. As this sold at 4/6 a tot, so increasing the bar's gross take and her commission, Ruth often ordered Pernod as an alternative to gin if a customer bought her a drink. The Pernod went down on top of the gin and even if mixing drinks does not make you drunk more quickly, it adds to the alcohol in the blood stream.

Ruth might have coped with the money worries if David had been content to drink only at the Little Club in the evenings but like most drinkers he moved from bar to bar and Ruth, increasingly possessive, as the carrot of matrimony seemed more accessible, would not let David out unaccompanied. So they went drinking elsewhere at other clubs, the Stirrup, the Steering Wheel, Esmeralda's – these were the most favoured. There was no 'slate' there, only cash, and David 'borrowed' from Ruth to pay.

These drinking forays in other clubs caused a reaction at the Little Club. Customers who had previously come to see Ruth were disappointed by her constant absence. They either left for good or did not spend as much money in the bar. This meant lower commission earnings on the drink sales for Ruth. The falling figures did not cheer Mr Conley and that was much more important. Morrie's bad temper worried Ruth and she increased her drinking to compensate for the additional worry. Often when she was in the Club, the barmaid would serve her water when she was drunk.

Whenever Ruth was in the Little Club she tried to regain lost business by flattering and flirting with the male customers. This infuriated David, who was as possessive and jealous as Ruth herself, and inevitably rows followed.

David too was drinking more heavily now. One reason was that the cycle of the Little Club and 'The Crown' public house and being drunk and hungover became a daily inevitability. His own awareness that he was in a terrible personal situation was also pushing up the drink level. Here he was 'stuck' with a woman older than himself, whose social class made marriage almost impossible, who expected him to fulfil those heady, alcoholic promises of eternal devotion, and was substantially keeping him.

Ruth's dilemma was equally unpleasant. Either she could cut loose from David and rebuild the club's business or she could gamble on getting out of club life altogether and achieving security and respectability by marrying David. She realized better than anyone that at twenty-eight time was against her.

Only mature human beings cope with unpleasant facts. Most console themselves with the idea that 'things will sort themselves out', and allow events to command their drifting lives.

This mixture of Micawber and Pangloss often works and the world is happily grateful. When events do not roughly cancel with each other to form a working life-pattern, but like a cancer, run wild through the structure of life, the result is often deadly. Neither David nor Ruth were mature enough personalities to make a decision about their problems, instead they allowed the Micawber-Pangloss philosophy to carry them willy-nilly to destruction.

Ruth's twenty-eighth birthday in October 1954 was the

excuse for one of those purposeless flashy parties she loved. Her birthday was on the ninth, but she decided to hold the party on the twelfth. David sent a greetings telegram from Penn and a birthday card whose choice would have discredited an insensitive *au pair* girl. It cost 5 1/2d, and on the front, which was Cambridge blue with white stippling around the edges, were two poorly drawn hands, one male, one female, the latter wearing a bracelet of pearls to avoid confusion. The hands held touching champagne glasses from which bubbles spattered the blue background. The caption at the top of the card read 'To you on your birthday'.

It was worse inside, where on the left, on a white background, nestling among red roses and some unrecognizable blue flowers were sheets of paper with the headings: 'Fortune', 'Health', 'True Friends'. (David had underlined 'true' three times), 'Joy and Good Cheer'. On the right hand side the doggerel on a white background read:

'Here's to your health—
May it always be good [four exclamation marks from
    David]
Here's to your plans [PARIS written in by David]
May they go as they should
Here's to good fortune [M. Cononley – wrongly spelt by
    David]
True friends and good cheer [Desmond and Gregg]
And to joy that increases Each day in the year.'

Underneath David had written: 'Sorry I couldn't find a better card, but in this part of the world they are unheard of. Happy birthday Darling, *BE GOOD*.
                    Love, David.'

It is impossible to believe that there was nothing less banal than this on sale at Penn. Ruth with her fervour for hoarding anything that anyone ever wrote to her, put the card away with the rest of the junk. No doubt she was pleased that David was jealous enough to keep harping about TRUE friends and BEING GOOD but a row came over her plans for Paris.

David had promised to take her there for a long weekend and he assured her that the plane tickets had been bought. Just before he had promised to collect her from the club to drive to the airport, he rang to say that 'all planes to and from Paris were grounded by fog'. Later when Ruth checked with the airport she discovered that this was a lie. David obviously could not afford the fares.

Other rows, fuelled by alcohol and shortage of money, increased and exploded in violence. David had always been aggressive when drunk but now, if he lost his temper with Ruth, he hit her.

Questioned by her Counsel at the Old Bailey Ruth Ellis described their relationship in the autumn of 1954.

Q. By October 1954 was there a further change in his behaviour towards you? How did he treat you physically?
A. He was violent on occasions.
Q. What sort of violence?
A. It was always because of jealousy in the bar. At the end of the evening when we got uptairs it was always about the things he had been seeing me do, and so on and so forth.
Q. How did this violence manifest itself?
A. He only used to hit me with his fists and his hands, but I bruise very easily, and I was full of bruises on many occasions.

Q. When he complained about your working in the club and exhibited this jealousy, how did you take it?

A. I often told him to please go, and not come back, sort of thing, but whether I meant it or not, I said it anyway.

Q. When you said that, did he ever go?

A. No.

Many have argued that as David Blakely was dead when this evidence was given it may not have been true and that Ruth Ellis was lying to obtain sympathy from the Court. This is wrong; if she were seeking to blacken David, why did she excuse his brutality by telling the Court 'I bruise very easily'? Secondly, there is unshakable independent evidence, not given in Court, of Blakely's physical violence.

A former member of the Little Club gives this comment on the situation in the autumn of 1954.

'Blakely often used to arrive intoxicated at seven o'clock in the evening and go on drinking. In this condition he was quarrelsome and aggressive towards everyone. Ruth Ellis was not aggressive. There were however, constant rows between them.

'I remember on one occasion about a month before Christmas, Blakely came into the Little Club about 8 pm in a bad temper. Ruth came in with Desmond having had some dinner with him. Blakely asked where she had been and she said she had just had dinner with Desmond. He said: "You're a liar, you have been sleeping with him". She said: "I'm not a liar and I do not like being called a liar, please go away". He went up to her and smacked her hard twice across the face. She was sitting down. I went to get hold of Blakely and she took hold of my hand and said: "No, let him alone", and took him upstairs. I heard several thumps. She came back at eleven o'clock and said she was fed up and wanted to leave him. She had been crying when she came back. I don't remember whether I saw bruises on that occasion but I have often seen them.'

The same witness described another incident in the club also just before Christmas 1954: 'Ruth was in the Little Club talking to a member and Blakely arrived about 6.30 pm dirty, unshaven and slightly under the influence of drink. He said: "I want to speak to you Ruth straight away", she said "Just a minute, I am busy, I am speaking to Brian." He grabbed her by the shoulder and pushed her out of the room and I heard the sound of a blow. She took him up to the flat and a few seconds afterwards I heard the sound of a blow and she fell down the stairs bruising herself severely. She told me that she never wanted to see him again but he kept ringing and ringing on the telephone and in the end she answered.'

How justifiable was Blakely's jealousy? Ruth was faithful to him in her fashion but she was still earning money by prostitution, although this was reduced by David's vigilant jealousy. A married man tells how at this period he picked Ruth Ellis up one night in a club, not the Little, and they went on a long drinking bout. 'Finally we went home, my wife was away at the time, to have a few more drinks. Ruth had been pretty moody all the evening and had refused to tell me what the trouble was.

'When we got home she suddenly started talking very excitedly and said "Do you know David Blakely the racing car driver?" I said I didn't and she then took off her clothes and I noticed that she was covered in bruises. I asked her what had happened and she told me that it "was David's work". I immediately asked her where this David lived, meaning to round there and give him a taste of his own medicine, but she wouldn't tell me. Finally she put on her clothes and I drove her to the Princess Beatrice Hospital in Finsborough Road, South Kensington. She went into the Casualty Department but after I had waited for a long time and she hadn't reappeared, I went in and they told me that she had refused to see anyone and had left by the front door.'

All this suggests that Ruth was either getting sexual satisfaction out of Blakely's ill treatment, or that she was prepared to put up with it as long as she thought he was serious about marrying her. The motive may have been a mixture of both, to which the indefinable word 'love' was added.

Another possibility is that Ruth may have felt that by letting David knock her about he would be satisfied that she was devoted to him and not probe her activities with other 'boy friends'. Even the most reconciled family would object to his marrying an ex-prostitute.

Whatever David's motives for hitting Ruth may have been, one cause was her own obsessive jealousy and nagging. Her husband, George Ellis, another heavy drinker, found this habit made him violent. Since the incident of the love bites Ruth had wanted to know how David spent every minute of the time he was away from her. She had heard from a member of the Little Club that David had once been in love with Mrs Findlater and there was a row over that between them. Finally, David had promised never to go to Tanza Road without telling her first, or taking her. This was no sacrifice, as he was unpopular with Carole for reasons which have already been explained.

By December 1954 business at the Little Club, according to figures Ruth wrote on scraps of paper and 'filed' away with love letters, visiting cards and diaries that she hoarded, showed takings of around £70–£80 a week. No matter what mark-up Morrie Conley put on the drinks, these takings could produce little profit. For months David had been complaining about Ruth working as a club manageress, trying as she put it 'to make me feel socially inferior to him'. When the inevitable break with Conley came Ruth had made her plans.

The faithful Cussen was her answer to the query of where to live without paying rent and at the same time providing a reasonable home for Andy when he came home for the Christmas holidays. It was Desmond himself who proposed it when Ruth had complained to him at the beginning of October about the difficulty of paying the rent for her flat.

Desmond suggested that she moved in to Goodwood Court with him. At the beginning of December, Ruth phoned Desmond to fix the deal. She then had to explain it to David, and he reacted with violent anger. Ruth pointed out that by giving up the flat she was making the first break with club life, something that David had been wanting her to do for months. In addition she was prepared to stop working in clubs altogether and to prove it she would leave the Little Club in the New Year; she was only staying on until Morrie could find a replacement. She told David not to worry about her living in the same flat as Desmond, because she and David could spend every night at a hotel if he wished. David swallowed all this specious reasoning because Ruth reminded him that if he really cared about her as he said, he could pay for somewhere to live and find enough money for her to stay at home like any other married or kept woman. It was unanswerable.

Although David had added to his income over the last

few months by selling secondhand motors on a commission basis for a Paddington dealer, he was still unable to keep Ruth. This 'job' of selling cars also had affected Ruth's relationship with the customers at the Little Club. People who were constantly pestered by Ruth 'to go and have a look at a bloody fine motor I've heard of' were unwilling to come into the club to be importuned to buy secondhand cars; too many customers were in the 'trade' themselves.

The 'sleeping out' system started almost as soon as Ruth moved to Goodwood Court. The hotel chosen was the Rodney, about a mile away from the Little Club, where they registered as Mr and Mrs Blakely, from Sheffield. Between 18 December 1954, and 4 February, 1955, inclusive, they stayed fifteen nights at the hotel. Normally they occupied room 71 which was booked by telephone; the charge was £3 a night.

Ruth and David usually arrived about midnight, went straight to bed, and after breakfast in their room would come down for a drink at the bar around 11 am. They seemed to the hotel staff like anyone who tips well and isn't sick in the foyer, 'a happy couple'.

At first the complaisant Cussen was told by Ruth that she was either staying the night with friends after a party, or visiting her child Georgina in the North. It was not until after Christmas that he found a hotel bill in the wastepaper basket at Goodwood Court that Ruth had forgotten to destroy. Normally David paid with his own money.

Christmas was no time of peace and good will. David was restless and sullen, drinking heavily and beginning to tell his friends that he wanted to leave Ruth. He explained to his friend Cliff Davis: 'I'd give anything to get away from her, but as soon as we meet it all starts again.' Ruth also confided in Cliff Davis about her certainty that David was unfaithful with other women. In her forceful, Brixton way she summed it up one night when they were drinking in Esmeralda's Club: 'I've given him some money and he's out somewhere, probably poking the arse off some tart.' It was clear that Mr Blakely's reservations about introducing Mrs Ellis to his family and upper-class friends in Bucks were not unfounded. He annoyed her too when he continually boasted: 'I am the social light of Buckinghamshire.' She felt that it was part of his policy of making her recognize her inferior class status.

David told Ruth that he was spending Christmas with his family, so she arranged a small Christmas Day party to which she invited the barmaid of the Little Club, Jackie Dyer, and a mutual friend, a businessman, Mr Bob Dykehouse. Ruth herself was happy enough that Christmas to joke with Mrs Dyer about her presents to David and Desmond. She had bought each man an identical silver cigarette case.

On Christmas night Ruth, Desmond, Mrs Dyer and Bob Dykehouse left Goodwood Court about 7 pm for a drink. As other guests were expected later a note was pinned to the door with the phone number of the club where they were drinking.

Ruth's son, Andy, was left alone in the flat. Soon after the party, David arrived, drunk, with a present for Andy, a toy revolver. David then phoned Ruth who, realizing he was tight, said that they would come back to the flat. The row started immediately, neither of them worrying that the boy could hear and see what was going on. As usual it was half a dozen of one and six of the other, each accusing the other of not telling the truth about what they had been doing in the pre-Christmas period. Each insinuated that the other had been unfaithful. David said: 'I am a poor twisted boy and she's the one that's made me so twisted. The girl I love sleeping with another man. It's her fault.' Ruth's written comment on the scene, made later, was an example of admirable understatement. 'It was most unpleasant, and completely spoiled the party.'

To avoid David babbling any more drunken truths Ruth bustled him downstairs into his car. There was another wrangle about what they should do, and in the end it was agreed that they should both go over to the Findlaters at Tanza Road. Desmond, who came down to see what was going on, followed them in his car as he was worried in case the drunken David should crash. The god who protects drunks driving motors was on duty and Desmond saw David's undamaged car parked outside the Findlaters' home.

The Findlaters were away staying in Bournemouth with relatives but David had a key to the flat and the reconciled couple spent the night there. When Ruth returned to Goodwood Court the next morning she told Desmond that she had been forced to stay with David as he had threatened to commit suicide if she left. Desmond, the devoted, accepted this excuse.

Whatever hangover, physical or emotional, David had the next morning, Boxing Day, it did not stop him driving the Emperor in its first race at Brand's Hatch. It came second in its event, the Kent Cup. *The Motor* magazine, reporting this race, said that the Emperor was 'an impressive challenger'.

On New Year's Eve, Ruth was reminded how difficult it would be to marry David, when he insisted that they went down to the 'Crown' at Penn to have a drink. Ruth had been there before and had been introduced to the landlord, Mr George Edward Swarbrick Beesley, who had accepted her as David's current girlfriend.

As David drove up to the pub he saw his mother going in and continued down the road to the next pub, the 'Red Lion'.

Here they had a few drinks with some of the staff of Silicon Pistons, David's firm, and then drove back to the 'Crown'. David went in first and then discovered that his mother was still in the bar so he brought Ruth a drink out to the car. He told her that when he kissed his mother and wished her a 'Happy New Year', she had said: 'How nice you smell.' Mrs Cook had caught the odour of some scent that Ruth had playfully dabbed behind David's ear before they left for Penn. To Ruth the news about the scent did not obscure the reality of her position: David was ashamed to take her into the pub to meet his mother. This irked her as she knew that the woman responsible for the love bites had been introduced to Mrs Cook. When David and Ruth drove back to London, Mrs Cook certainly did not suspect that her son's current mistress had been waiting, like a child with a bag of crisps and a bottle of pop, outside the pub.

At the start of the New Year both David and Ruth were telling the same story to their friends, he that he wanted to leave her but that she would not let him, and she saying the same thing about him.

Whatever he said publicly, David was still showing acute jealousy in private. When they were not at the Rodney Hotel together David would ring up from Penn to Goodwood Court. The first call would be about 10 pm and the second at 1 am. Ruth inevitably asked him where he was phoning from at one in the morning and David invariably said from the phone box by the Post Office. Ruth would ask what he was doing there at that time of night. David's reply was that he was on his way home from the Penn night club. Ruth, who had visited every drinking outlet in the neighbourhood with David, wanted to know where this was. David, who could never keep a discreet tongue, confessed that after the Crown closed he would go with friends to drink with them at the home of one of the party. He was stupid enough to name the house.

One night David phoned as the 'Crown' was closing and told Ruth that he was going home to bed to have an early night. This is Ruth's account of what happened then: 'I then got my coat and I told Desmond that I wanted to catch David out once and for all and that I wanted him to drive me to Penn. I went straight to David's garage and his car was not there. I watched [the house David had called the Penn night club], he came out of there at about 2.30 as he always did. I said next day: "How do you feel after your early night?" and he said "Awful". I never mentioned the fact that I had been watching him.'

Ruth soon discovered that what she called 'the attraction' was a very good-looking married woman, who, inevitably, was older than David. He spent much time in the lunch hour 'session' drinking and playing darts with her at the 'Crown'. She also found out that the woman's husband was often away from home.

Naturally Ruth was not silent for long and she demanded to meet the woman in David's presence. This he put off with excuses or, when they did go down to the 'Crown', he chose times when he knew that the other woman would not be there.

Despite her suspicions Ruth was still willing to spend

nights with David at the Rodney Hotel. (The fact that on some occasions Desmond was away or came in very late and Andy had to fend for himself never worried her. She would do anything for Andy except inconvenience herself.) They stayed at the hotel on the night of 8 January and they had a row which was worse than normal. The subject was the lady at Penn and in his usual little-boy-tell-the-truth-and-all-will-be-well fashion David admitted that he had often kissed the lady of Penn. One of David's taunts during this row particularly annoyed Ruth. Two days previously her friend and companion call-girl Vicki Martin had been killed in a car crash. 'That's how you'll end up,' David had said.

The next day David returned to Penn, the row apparently forgotten. He did not phone either at lunch time or bedtime. By 10 January Ruth was in a passion of jealousy and had phoned him at home to say that she was coming down to Penn to have it out with the woman and tell David's mother all about it. She reinforced this by a telegram, dictated over Desmond's phone to David at Silicon Pistons. It read: 'PERSONAL MR D AND D BLAKELEY [*sic*] SYLICUM PISTONS LTD PENN BUCKS HAVENT YOU GOT THE GUTS TO SAY GOODBYE TO MY FACE – RUTH.'

David was frightened that Ruth would rouse a local scandal, and that all the old trouble about him spending too much time at the 'Crown' would come up again between him and his family. There was also the lady of Penn's husband to consider. He was terrified too that Ruth might get some of her London gangster friends to drop around and have a friendly chat, a possibility she had mentioned in one of their previous rows. David had a talk with the landlord of the 'Crown' and asked him whether he should go to the lady of Penn and tell all: wisely Mr Beesley told him to sleep on it. David stayed silent. He then asked Ant Findlater for advice, who said that he and Ruth had better agree to live reasonably together or not at all. David assured Ant that what he really wanted to do was to get away from Ruth and never see her again. Nevertheless by 14 January they were back fighting in Room 71 of the Rodney Hotel and when they went to a dance at Richmond, David had to cover the bruises on Ruth's shoulders with make-up.

Desmond was disappointed that Ruth and David were back together although at this time he did not know, or preferred not to realize, that they were regularly sleeping together. During the row with David, Ruth had assured Desmond that she was finished with David, 'the cheapest of cheap-skates', for ever. The assurance was qualified by Ruth's continued off-key singing all over the flat of 'I still believe we were meant for each other', a record David had just given her.

Desmond's attitude was that there was no harm in David and Ruth meeting, especially as Ruth had told him that she was trying hard to break free from David.

Between fights, Ruth had decided to learn French, naturally at Desmond's expense, and her first tutor had been a French-born photographer but David was so jealous that she engaged a Frenchwoman. The reason for these lessons was to enable her to shine when she accompanied David to France later that year for the Le Mans racing. He was to be a member of the 'Bristol' team. Her progress was nil. Ruth was seldom at Goodwood Court when the tutor called and when she was at home she was in such a highly tense and nervous condition that she could not concentrate. Ruth chain-smoked all the time during the lessons and continually offered the tutor drinks, which she refused. Ruth herself did not drink in the tutor's presence.

Ruth explained the lack of concentration and obvious nervous tension to her tutor as the result of the endless cavalcade of parties and dinners that she and her fiancé gave and attended. In fact, Ruth and David were at the nadir of their affair. She knew that he was only attached to her by fear and dying lust, for his infidelity was proven by events at Penn.

Her nagging, her possessive jealousy, and her brand of love became more strident. As she mooned and drank at Goodwood Court she continually sang 'I still believe we were meant for each other'. Wishing, as another favourite pop song of Ruth's declared 'Would Make It So'.

Reality intruded on 14 January 1955, when a *decree nisi* was granted to George Ellis; in three months she would be free and David could marry her. By the end of January David had still not made a definite proposal and Ruth attacked him on a front on which she could always attain a tactical success.

Ruth and David went on a drink and sex spree that started on 27 January and ended in the hysterics of exhaustion on 6 February. Sometimes she would return to Goodwood Court to change her clothes and spend the night there, but most nights she stayed with David at the Rodney and another unidentified hotel. Her excuses to Desmond varied from going out to the theatre with her husband, George Ellis, to travelling north to see Georgina. On Monday, 31 January, she was back at Goodwood Court and Desmond found a torn hotel bill in the name of Mr and Mrs Blakely in her jacket pocket. That week she spent two more nights with David at the Rodney Hotel on the excuse that she was visiting a sick girlfriend. Desmond frequently saw her in the Steering Wheel drinking with David and other friends but he did not challenge them. Instead he drove past the Rodney Hotel on the Friday evening, 4 February, and saw David's car parked there. It was there when he returned from a trip out of London on Sunday morning so he decided not to go back to his flat. Ruth described what happened when she and David returned to Goodwood Court that evening.

David and I had been out drinking, and had been drinking quite a lot, and we got back to Desmond's flat expecting David to drop me off there, but David did not want to. There was a scene again, and I think he realized that he had gone too far. I had really been hurt; and then he pushed off and phoned − I did not know he had phoned at the time, but I discovered afterwards he apparently went to a phone − and said "Will you come and get me?". Something like that. I do not know what he said.'

David phoned Ant Findlater's flat, but Ant was out with a friend, Clive Gunnell, who had helped with the Emperor which was now kept at the garage where Gunnell worked, No. 12 Rex Place, Mayfair. Carole Findlater answered the phone and David, sounding very agitated, left Desmond's number with the request that Ant phoned as soon as he returned. After speaking to David, Ant and Clive motored hard from Hampstead to Goodwood Court in Marylebone. The message which set these two off so promptly to rescue their friend from his mistress was: 'She's taken the keys to my car, will you come and get me?' It does not seem to have occurred to David that he could either have walked away or taken a bus or taxi. When Ant and Gunnell arrived both David and Ruth were drunk. There had been a tremendous fight. Ruth had a black eye and was limping. David had a black eye too and he told Ant: 'She's an absolute bitch, she tried to knife me.' He showed Ant a long scratch on his arm. The fight was started by jealousy. Ruth accused David of an affair at Penn (which was true), and he had riposted that she was sleeping with Desmond (which was also true).

He was eager to get away from Ruth, who, despite her physical wounds, was still mastered by her jealous possessiveness. To stop him running away, Ruth had taken his keys, knowing that David would never leave his treasured motor and walk.

While Ant and Clive examined Ruth's bruises, David found the car keys and slipped out of the flat and went downstairs to his car. Ruth suddenly noticed that David had gone and was waiting for his friends on the pavement. She ran after David. In the street there was a hysterical scene from Ruth who realized that David was seriously trying to leave her. He kept saying: 'She won't let me go.' She turned to Ant and Clive with the heavy sarcasm of the drunk and said: 'What a hero he is to need two great big men like you to come and rescue him from a mere woman.'

To stop David leaving she sat in the driving seat of his car. Ant, David and Gunnell then got into Ant's car. Ruth lurched out of David's car and leaned through the window of Ant's motor, stopping him driving off.

The three men got out of the car and Clive tried to calm the hysterical Ruth. Ant told David to get into his own car and drive off while Ruth's attention was diverted. David did so and the two men then got into their car. Screaming, Ruth lay down in front of Ant's motor. The tiresome negotiations for peace began all over again, ending when Ruth joined the two men in a cup of coffee at a café. Afterwards Ant and Clive drove her back to Goodwood Court.

By the time Ruth got back Desmond was home; as she limped around the flat she told him that the black eye and bruises were the result of a fight in which David had kicked and beaten her. She did not tell Desmond of the damage she had done to David. Ruth mentioned to Desmond that there had been a lot of drinking over the past few days, and she hobbled to bed to sleep it off.

Back at Tanza Road David removed his shirt in front of Mrs Findlater; his back was a mass of welts and bruises.

Ruth awoke about 10 pm; the knowledge that David had escaped and had said he was not coming back, began another phase of neurotic, possessive jealousy. The obliging Desmond, who knew that she and David were sleeping together regularly, was ordered to take her on a car hunt for David. First they went to Tanza Road and saw David, Clive and the Findlaters leaving by car for the 'Magdala' public house, three-quarters of a mile away. Ruth said: 'Oh, he must have boys with him to protect him,' but did not go into the pub and make David apologize, which was her reason for the trip.

Instead she and Desmond waited in the car until closing time, when all of David's party came out of the pub and David drove off alone. Desmond suggested that David was going home to Penn, but Ruth was convinced that he was off to spend the night with another woman. Back at Desmond's flat, Ruth phoned a friend for the address of the woman David had named to Ruth as the originator of the love bites on his back. She lived in Gower Street, near Euston Station, but when they arrived they found that it was the wrong address and there was no sign of David's car in any nearby street. Undaunted, Ruth decided to go to Penn where they arrived in the early hours of Monday morning.

Ruth hobbled down the drive at the Old Park and went to the door of David's flat. His nanny came to the door first and then David appeared in his pyjamas. David was clearly frightened that either the noise would wake the rest of the house or that Ruth would use the carving knife on him again. He bolted out of the door and into his car. Eventually David drove back, swung into the drive, and by the time Ruth had fumbled back to the door, David was inside. This time nobody answered her ringing and knocking so she returned to London, complaining constantly of the pain in her ankle.

At the flat Desmond helped her to bed and noticed that she had bruises all over her body. Ruth stayed awake and refused breakfast and Desmond suggested that she should go to the Middlesex Hospital for an examination of her ankle. But Ruth wanted to return to Penn 'to get an apology from that bastard'.

Before they left Ruth rang David at his work, but he was 'not available', so Desmond took the phone and said 'it would be to Mr Blakely's own good to answer the call'. Mr Blakely decided that he would be better off not coming to the phone.

They left London at about 11 am and *en route* for Penn saw David's car outside the 'Bull' at Gerrards Cross, a pub where Ruth and David were well known to the cocktail bar attendant, Mr Dennis Tovell. Desmond parked his car, and leaving Ruth in it, went inside. David was sitting at the bar drinking, chatting to the barman. Desmond grabbed David by his jacket and said: 'Come on you bastard, outside.'

Outside Desmond told David that he must apologize to Ruth and David said: 'What am I supposed to say?' Desmond replied: 'Do you normally go around knocking women about? As far as I'm concerned she has every right to take police action against you.'

David walked over to Ruth, who was still sitting in the car and said: 'I'm sorry, Ruth.'

This did not impress Desmond who was by now suffused with jealous anger. He said to David: 'Well, here's your opportunity, what about hitting a man instead of a woman?' David said: 'Oh, you're stronger than I am. I wouldn't fight you, you're bigger than I am anyway.' This was untrue, but David was a physical coward.

Desmond, conscious that Ruth was watching and listening, called David a 'gutless little bastard'. Ruth added her verbal left hook by saying to David: 'This is no good. I am going to see your mother.' As always this scared David and he apologized again. Ruth was as angry as Desmond and she yelled: 'What about all the money you owe me?'

David replied: 'Ruth, I thought it was an agreement when we went out we should always go dutch?' Then, remembering the bills she had paid for him at the Little Club and the other money she had lent him, David added:

'And what about all your money you keep talking about?'

Ruth countered by saying: 'You've broken my ankle, and I'm going to see your mother about it.'

David decided to run and said: 'I've got an appointment in London, and you've made me late already.' He walked to his car and drove off. Desmond and Ruth took the Penn road.

On the way to Penn, Desmond, very reasonably in the circumstances, pointed out to Ruth that she had got what she came for, an apology from David, so what was the use of causing family bickering by seeing Mrs Cook? Ruth agreed that telling David's mother would do no good; it

Ruth at Brands Hatch with David and a friend.

Mrs Gladys Kensington Yule, a passer-by who was hit in the thumb by one of the six bullets fired at David.

The Magdala Public House outside which Ruth shot her lover, David Blakely.

The Findlaters' second floor flat at No. 29 Tanza Road, Hampstead.

Ruth cried in court when this photograph of David was handed to her.

Desmond Cussen, the company director with whom Ruth lived after she left the 'Little Club'.

*(left to right)* Carole and 'Ant' Findlater with Ruth and David in the 'Little Club'.

Ruth with friends at The Dorchester. Desmond is on her right.

Ruth Ellis and David Blakely in the bar at the 'Little Club' where Ruth was manageress.

Ruth with Desmond Cussen, her 'alternative lover'.

Ruth embarked on an unsuccessful modelling career.

would only decrease her chances of being accepted as David's wife. She still wanted to go to the police. Desmond argued that this must involve the family and probably her own child. (During all the upset of the weekend, nobody ever mentioned Andy when recalling the facts, but he may have been a witness to the fighting at the flat.) Finally Ruth agreed to return to London and have her ankle examined at the Middlesex Hospital. This was on 7 February. The ankle was X-rayed and, though severely bruised, was unbroken. When they returned to the flat, Ruth's mother and father were there and she told them that she had had an accident, a story that did not convince them.

Later that day a bunch of red carnations arrived with a card enclosed: 'Sorry darling, I love you, David.' It is guesswork whether love, or fear that Penn would be scandalized, produced the reconciliation; my guess is fear.

When they met in the evening, David said his violence was the result of the frustration of knowing that Ruth was sharing a flat with Desmond. Ruth was always eager to control David's movements and so she suggested that they should live together. David, unwilling to be supervised, but with no money left to pay for regular visits to the Rodney, could not make up his mind. Finally Ruth persuaded David that she knew someone who would lend her the money for the rent, which David could repay when the Emperor was marketed. What she did not say was that she had decided to borrow the money from Desmond.

At Goodwood Court Ruth explained to Desmond that she was moving, as it was unfair to keep involving Desmond in scenes when David called.

Obligingly Desmond agreed to lend her the rent money and Ruth promised to come round and cook for him, a compromise that meant she kept a set of keys to Goodwood Court.

The next morning, 8 February, Ruth bought an early edition of the *Evening Standard* and took a taxi to No. 44 Egerton Gardens, an architecturally abominable street of tall, red brick houses opposite Brompton Oratory in Kensington. The house consisted of fourteen furnished service rooms and was managed by a resident housekeeper, Mrs Joan Ada Georgina Dayrell Winstanley, middle-aged, tough but kindly, who had once owned a club in South Kensington. Ruth introduced herself as Mrs Ellis and said that she would be occupying the room with her husband who was 'in the motor world'. Ruth asked Mrs Winstanley to rearrange the furniture and to lend her a flower vase. Her husband, she explained, was very particular about always having flowers in the room. Ruth paid a week's rent of six guineas in advance on room number 5. Next day, 9 February, Mr and Mrs Ellis moved in. With extras, and breakfast in bed, the bill was around £7 a week. It was not long before a man was calling after 'Mr Ellis' had left for work. Mrs Winstanley discovered that his name was Mr Cussen.

It was unlikely that the move to Egerton Gardens would resolve the dangerous tension between Ruth and David. On his side, he had tried to break with her twice since Christmas and on both occasions she had got him back principally by threats to involve his family and friends in Penn. The last row when she tried to kill him with a carving knife, as well as bruising him badly, had terrified David. Mrs Findlater noticed the change in David after this incident. He began to look scared. David also told the Findlaters that after one row between himself and Ruth, he had returned to Culross Street, where he was attacked by unidentified men. He ran into the house but he was certain that the men were gangster friends of Ruth and that she was fulfilling her promise to turn the 'boys' on him if he left her. David may have invented the incident but certainly Ruth was capable of it; the names in her address books of men with known criminal records proves that she had the means to fulfil the threat. David was now telling his friends, including the lady at Penn, that Ruth 'is madly in love with me, but I hate her guts'.

About ten days after she moved to Egerton Gardens, Ruth decided to become a model, an occupation that seemed both socially respectable and profitable. She did not consider the fact that she had no qualifications, her legs were too bowed and skinny, and her posing was giraffe-like. Her enormous vanity convinced her that these disadvantages did not matter. Desmond, who when he was not chauffeuring Ruth, was a very practical businessman, said: 'If you're going in for modelling, you can't afford to get yourself knocked about and bruised.' Ruth optimistically replied: 'Oh no, he's promised to be good now.'

They went to the Marjorie Molyneux modelling school to inquire about a course. Here Ruth was interviewed and tactfully told that 'you have a very attractive walk' and she could join the next course on 7 March. The fee of twenty guineas was paid by Desmond, but the money was repaid by Ruth. She explained that she had 'borrowed' it from one of her married boyfriends. She was obviously still in business.

Although Ruth realized that David must spend some time with his family for the sake of appearances, she could not control her jealous tongue and there were soon rows about what he did on the nights he was at Penn.

On 22 February, the inevitable row over the woman at

Penn erupted at Egerton Gardens. There was a fight in which Ruth was severely bruised about the shoulders and got a slight black eye. Later when Desmond faced David about this, David admitted striking Ruth but claimed that this time it was self-defence as Ruth had swung at him with a gin bottle.

After this, on whim or suspicion, Ruth was chauffeured by Desmond and shadowed David constantly to work, while he was playing darts at the 'Crown', and also tracked him to his home at Penn. At the end of February, Ruth and Desmond waited all night outside the house of the married woman at Penn with whom Ruth knew David was sleeping.

At nine next morning David left her house, saw Desmond's car, and ran back inside where the married woman said: 'What are you frightened of?'

David said: 'I didn't think they would carry it as far as that.'

Ruth said to Desmond as David ran: 'If that's not guilt I don't know what is.'

David came out, after Desmond had knocked on the door, and Ruth demanded to know what had happened. He explained that he had stayed the night after a party.

Ruth replied: 'You look as though you've had a party all right, but not the sort you brag about. Just look at your eyes.'

David drove off to work but later Ruth returned and spoke to the 'other woman'. She came to the door and after Ruth had quietly apologized for 'so much trouble' invited her in for coffee. This is Ruth's account of the meeting: 'I explained the situation and she said: "I'm very sorry, it is all my fault. I did not know David had anything so important in London." I said I could not understand why he spent the night there when his home was only just up the road. She said "He is not very happy at home." Knowing David like I do, I know for a fact he would not have spent the night there for nothing. An attractive woman on her own who's [*sic*] husband was always away. Later on I discovered that they both contradicted one another's stories.'

After this Ruth left the house and went to have a few drinks at the 'Crown' with Desmond. It was opening time by now and like all alcoholics she needed topping up for the day. Ruth 'phoned David from the pub at the works and got Desmond to speak to him. David said: 'Do you want to make a court case out of it?' (the assault on Ruth).

Desmond replied: 'Don't be ridiculous – come down here and have a drink, I won't hit you.'

David arrived about lunch time with his employer and the married woman. He was making sure that he had someone to protect him in case Desmond changed his mind.

Ruth went to the 'Crown' at lunch time to find David. A wrangle began over the British Racing Drivers' Club dance that was being held at the Hyde Park Hotel that evening. Ruth, who had asked David to take her and been told that he was not going, had arranged to be partnered by Desmond. Now at the pub David said: 'I'll see you at the dance.' Ruth said angrily: 'You knew you were going all the time, you're just trying to annoy me.' David went out of the pub.

After more drinks, Desmond left Ruth in the 'Crown' and went to the works and saw David privately. He apologized 'for our odd behaviour in following you about'. David accepted the gesture and Desmond asked: 'Would it embarrass you further if Ruth and I went to the dance tonight?' David said: 'No'. The two men shook hands and Desmond left to collect Ruth. On the journey to London, she stopped to phone David yet again at the works but did not tell Desmond what they had discussed. On the way back Ruth was in what Desmond described as 'a pretty upset condition' but she went to her hairdresser, Shack's, in Shaftesbury Avenue, to get ready for the dance. After she had finished at Shack's, Desmond drove her to Egerton Gardens and then, as she had eaten nothing all day, and there was no food in the house, drove over to his flat, made some sandwiches and brought them back for her. Ruth was still getting ready for the dance when he returned and he helped her cover up the bruises on her shoulders with make-up. Suddenly, while they were eating. Ruth said: 'I don't know whether I love him, or I am going mad.' Desmond, who was tired, did not pay much attention and said: 'You're all right, Ruth, you're a bit overwrought.'

Desmond and Ruth did not go direct from Goodwood Court to the Hyde Park Hotel; first they had drinks at the Steering Wheel Club in Brick Street, about a mile from the hotel. At the Hyde Park Hotel an agitated David was continually leaving his party to telephone various drinking clubs to inquire whether Ruth was there. David had not asked Ruth to join his party because it included his mother and stepfather; he was not risking trouble. Nevertheless, as the evening wore on, and he had enough drink, his jealousy of Ruth and Desmond overcame caution about his family.

He met her in the foyer as Desmond was putting his coat away and he asked sharply: 'Where have you been all this time?' When Desmond joined them, he tackled him: 'You arrived very late, where have you been all this time?' Desmond replied: 'Her ladyship was kept a long time at the hairdressers.' They went into the ballroom and for the next hour or so Ruth danced first with Desmond and then with David.

According to Ruth, David was being 'extremely funny and very rude to people all the evening'. Desmond noted that they seemed on the best of terms. This atmosphere of rude and amusing conviviality dulled a little around midnight when Desmond bought a bottle of champagne and Ruth suggested that they should drink a toast to her divorce which she said 'has been made absolute today'. In fact it had not, and was not made absolute until later in March. Either Ruth was lying to see what David's reaction was, or in her perpetual state of drunken mental muddle, she had genuinely mixed up the date. Whatever the motive for the toast the result must have depressed her. David refused to drink with them.

He had again done the worst possible thing – he had hardened the idea that had been sickening her for some time: David Blakely had no intention of marrying her. He was using her and making a fool of her. The dance ended in the early morning and Ruth and Desmond began to say their goodbyes. This is Ruth's account of what happened. 'As I said good-night, to people I knew, he [David] said: "I will see you later" and sure enough he was in bed next morning when I woke up. [Desmond had dropped her off at Egerton Gardens after the dance.] I said "After your last night [the affair at Penn] I don't know how you have the nerve to be here." He said "You know I will always come back to you."

'David and I separated for a week after this but I continued going around with Desmond to the usual bars we drank in. [She also started the modelling course to which Desmond drove her every morning and collected her in the afternoon. The new clothes for the course were paid for by Desmond.] David would not give me back the keys so I got Desmond to get the keys back from him which he did. [Desmond's account of the recovery of the keys was that he went to the Steering Wheel Club and told David to come outside. Whereupon he knocked David down and Ruth snatched the keys from David's key ring. During the argument, Desmond said 'David you are nothing but a ponce' – an accusation which David countered by saying: 'If I had known that you paid the rent at 44 I would have killed her.' As it was dangerous to fulfil this threat with Desmond around, who was quite willing to knock him down again, David dusted off his suit and went in to the club for another drink.]

'At a later date I was drinking at the Stirrup Club, talking to some people, I had left my bag at the end of the bar, David walked in, he opened my bag without asking me and said he was looking for his key. I said: "Leave my bag alone." I cannot remember whether I smacked him round the mouth or not, I seem to think I did. He left the bar. When I got back to Egerton Gardens I found him outside. I said "What are you doing here?" He said: "You said if I stopped the affair at Penn everything would be all right." I said: "Have you?" He said: "Yes."

'I believed him. He seemed so genuine and sincere. Later on, he said "I have been wanting to come home to you all the week, it's been hell. I have missed you so much. I have slept with you so long I cannot sleep without you." I said "That is no excuse for sleeping with somebody else".'

This, of course, is Ruth's side of the story and may not be true. Her accounts of the conversation read true. Then there is Blakely's reluctance to give up the keys to No. 44, not the reaction of a man who was desperately trying to get away.

Whatever David may have felt he ought to do he obviously found, after a few days away from Ruth, that his sexual compulsions drove him back. At this time too Ruth had discovered an important reason why David should be forgiven and encouraged to come home. She was pregnant.

The day after the reconciliation David left for Penn about 8.15. This is Ruth's account of what she did: 'It was a beautiful day so I decided to go to the "Crown" in Penn for lunch. So Desmond drove me there. I also wanted to see if David was telling the truth. I walked in and David was there with . . .; when I walked in he looked very guilty, walked over and bought me a drink. He said "I must go." As he got to the door . . . said: "David you will drop that chair off for me won't you?" He just did not know which way to look. He said: "Yes." [Ruth's reporting of this incident is very accurate and has been confirmed by an independent witness.]

'I told him once again what I thought of him, on the telephone, but he arrived back full of excuses. He said: "I cannot help it if she goes into the 'Crown'." I said "It seems one cannot walk in there without finding you with her there. What do you do when your mother comes through?" He said ". . . and I go into the darts room." I said: "A very well organized set-up, making your mother a fool to the rest of Penn." He said: "They all know what my mother is like." I said "I don't believe your mother is as bad as that." He said "That's because you have never met her."

'I said later, a few days later, "You never mention . . . husband, don't you ever see him?" He said "He comes home nights and at weekends." I said "It seems funny you spend the day with her and then at night you come to London when he arrives in Penn, weekends you spend with me when her husband is home. It is no good David, in my condition at this moment I cannot stand all this, I am feeling ill, you will have to go out of my life."

'He then smacked me on the cheek with his fist clenched. I saw stars, my ear was tingling and I had seemed to have gone deaf. He then put his two fingers around my throat, with the other hand he punched me in the stomach. I was crying, his fingers pressed tightly around my throat and everything went black. He was like a mad man, the expression on his face was frightening. He said "Oh God don't let me do it." He repeated it. My throat felt swollen and I was having difficulty in swallowing. I was coughing. In between these bouts I said "You are mad, you are stark raving mad." He said "One of these days I will kill you." I said "You have done that already."'

It is now impossible to say whether at this time David Blakely knew that Ruth was pregnant but if he did, and what Ruth says about hitting her in the stomach is true, then it was despicable. At the Old Bailey her counsel, Mr Melford Stevenson, tried to show that a miscarriage resulted from this fight, but Ruth hedged.

He asked her: In March did you find that you were pregnant?

A. Yes.
Q. At the end of March did you do anything about that pregnancy; what happened about it?
A. Well, we had a fight a few days previously – I forget the exact time – and David got very, very violent. I do not know whether that caused the miscarriage or not, but he did thump me in the tummy.
Q. And that was followed by a miscarriage?
A. Yes.

After the miscarriage she wrote: 'On the 28 March, I had an abortion and I was not at all well. On that occasion David took no interest in my welfare and did not even bother to inquire if I was all right. I was very hurt indeed about this and I began to feel a growing contempt for him. The results of my abortion, in fact, continued until Tuesday, 5 April.'

David's attitude from the beginning, according to Ruth, had been equally unsatisfactory. At first he told her that there was no question of having the child, it was economically impossible. Then he changed his mind and said they should have it. This change of mind was accompanied by the tasteless remark 'Oh well I can just about afford seven shillings a week.' Ruth unjustifiably blamed this and 'all kinds of other nasty remarks' on the Findlaters, whom she had told that she was pregnant.

Certainly the Findlaters, especially Carole, did not believe Ruth, and regarded it as a trick to make David marry her. David and Ant had also discussed the possibility that the child might not be David's; she had been living with Desmond until the beginning of February. As with her pregnancy the previous Christmas, the identity of the father is based on Ruth's word.

# 6

## The Week of Decision

On Saturday, 2 April, the Emperor had been entered for a race at Oulton Park, a track near Chester. Ruth was anxious that David should be fit for the race and the proposals that she made to him were sensible ones: 'I said, "I think you drink too much David, you must stop drinking so much. In fact, we'll both stop drinking." He said "All right, just the occasional one."

'I said: "Anyway you must get fit for the race." All that week he worked late on the car. He arrived home about 12. 30-1 o'clock, very dirty, smothered in grease and oil. Anthony and David, Dennis and Clive [two friends] worked hard to get the car ready for the race. I was in bed early all that week, he used to phone from Rex Place and check to see if I was in bed like I promised.

'Wednesday night [29 March, the day after the abortion] he arrived home earlier than usual. He said they had put the racing car in the garage of his mother's flat in Culross Street. He said "What do you think darling?" I said: "Now what's happened?" He said: "Well, Ant and I and Clive and Dennis were putting the car in the garage when my mother came down and invited us all up for a drink. She was in a very good mood." I said "I am very pleased, that makes us all very happy."

'Then he said: "I wish we had enough money, we could have kept our little David. I didn't want you to get rid of it." He was then very concerned and said: "Everything will turn out all right. No one is ever going to part us. I do love you so much Ruth."

'The following morning I had prepared a picnic basket, smoked salmon sandwiches and a whole chicken, box of biscuits, sweets and chocolates for David because he liked chocolates while he was driving, also a flask of tea. That day previously I had bought him his new gloves for wearing while driving his racing car.'

These were string-backed gloves and David had asked Ruth to buy them for him. He had now come to accept that she should buy things like shoes and gloves. Ruth revealed later that 'he forgot to say thank you for the gloves'.

Before they left for Oulton Park, Ruth phoned several friends and said that things had improved between herself and David and they would be getting married soon.

On Thursday David, Dennis, Ant and Ruth departed for Chester. David drove the Emperor and Ant had David's Vanguard brake. Desmond had gone to Wales for the week-end, and Ruth had 'forgotten' to tell him she was going away with David. She was not feeling well, for she was still losing blood after the abortion. On Thursday night she and David stayed at a hotel in Chester as Mr and Mrs Blakely. The next day, Friday, it was raining hard and despite her illness Ruth went with David to the track at Oulton Park to watch him drive the Emperor on a practice run.

In its April 1955 issue the magazine *Lilliput* had a special, illustrated article on the car called 'Building a 130mph Special'. The unnamed author wrote 'In the final count the Emperor may crash before it can prove itself (there is no second string to the stable) it may flop or it may become a sensation. Motor racing is too chancy to predict the outcome.'

It was an accurate comment, for while practising the car broke down and was a write-off for Saturday's racing.

Carole Findlater, who was now Woman's Editor of the *Daily Mail*, had been driven up by a friend on the paper and arrived at Chester on the Friday night to find everyone 'in the dumps' over the car. It was agreed that they would stay on for the racing on Saturday and return to London on Sunday morning.

On Friday night David and Ruth had a quarrel over the car. David in the fury of his disappointment had said to Ruth 'It's all your fault, you jinxed me.' He was recalling what Ruth had once told him. 'You will never have any luck the way you treat me.' According to Ruth, David then said 'All right, so I'm no good. I'm a rotter, but they all love me.' Ruth said 'I'll stand so much from you David, you cannot go on walking over me for ever.' He said: 'You'll stand it because you love me.'

After the first surge of anger over the broken-down car at Oulton David said, according to Ruth: 'I have asked for bad luck, now I have got it.'

Ruth assumed that this meant that David was sorry about the way he had treated her. It may equally have meant he felt that he had courted bad luck by living with her. Ruth's reply to David was 'You cannot go on playing dirty tricks on people and getting away with it.'

On the Saturday night, after the racing, the Findlaters, David, Ruth and Dennis had a party in the hotel bar. Ruth was surly and Mrs Findlater recalls that she was 'sitting there like the Snow Queen', quite uninterested in the car and continually niggling because her champagne had not arrived. David kept saying 'I can't afford to get the car repaired.'

That Saturday Desmond Cussen returned from Wales to find a telegram at Goodwood Court saying that Andy's school was due to break up that day. Ruth had apparently forgotten this, and she had also not informed the school of her new address. Desmond phoned Ruth at Egerton Gardens to tell her about Andy but Mrs Winstanley, the housekeeper, said that 'Mrs Ellis had gone North to see her husband motor racing.' Mrs Winstanley then discovered a note left by Ruth saying that if Mr Cussen rang would she please tell him that Mrs Ellis would phone him on Monday morning. There was nothing Desmond could do.

Ruth and the dejected party from Chester arrived back in London on Sunday night. She had caught a severe cold while watching David practise in the rain the previous Friday and she was feverish with this and the effects of her abortion. She was also extremely depressed by an incident with David just before they left the hotel.

David had told her that he had not enough money to pay the bill, so she lent him £5. On her way downstairs to the car she saw him at the desk signing a cheque for the bill. At the Old Bailey Mr Stevenson asked her: 'What effect did it have on you?' She answered: 'I just thought it was a mean way of getting money from me when he had sufficient to pay the bill himself, or appeared to have.'

If David had explained to her that he wanted £5 because he had no ready cash, she would have given it to him. What infuriated her was that she had been 'conned' out of the money; it was another proof to her that she could now not believe anything he said.

It was a slow journey to London with the broken-down Emperor towed by the Vanguard, and after garaging the car everyone had a drink. Ruth was so depressed that she got drunk and was taken home and put to bed by David. When Desmond came round the next morning, he took her temperature. It was 104°, and he insisted that she stayed in bed while he went to Aylesbury to fetch Andy. When the boy arrived home, he was given a camp bed to sleep on in the same room as Ruth and David.

When later she recalled the effect that the weekend had on their relationship she wrote: 'I used to be good company and fun to be with. He had turned me into a surly, miserable woman. I was growing to loathe him, he was so conceited and said that all women loved him. He was so much in love with himself.'

Now began the decisive week. Although she was ill, she could not stay in that furnished bedsitting room, and on nearly every day in the coming week she would go round to Desmond's flat at lunch time to prepare a meal for herself and Andy, and sometimes one for Desmond. On both the Monday and Tuesday David had told her that he was seeing someone about the car; and he had arrived at Egerton Gardens very late.

Ruth later wrote: 'It was either on the Monday or the Tuesday night that I discovered that David was at the Steering Wheel spending my money on a party of friends without me.' She was still annoyed about the £5 that she had given David on the Sunday night.

At the Old Bailey Mr Stevenson asked her what were her reactions when she discovered that David was drinking at the Steering Wheel without her. She said: 'I felt nothing but contempt for him.' This was her usual reaction when she was cross with David; she described him as 'a drip', a 'conceited little bastard' and 'the lowest of the low'.

Ruth was unfair to David over the events of Monday and Tuesday. He had told her that he was seeing someone about the car and she knew that this meant they would meet either in a club or a pub. David was very worried about the car and was trying to find out from friends in the trade the cost of repairs, or what he could sell it for. In addition, he cannot have been eager to go home to a bedsitting room in which world-wise Andy had a camp bed. Ruth did not or would not understand any of these points. What angered her was that he should have the impudence to go out without her, even though she was going out with Desmond. This attitude was normal for Ruth, but it was accentuated by her severe chill and the abortion.

On Wednesday night, David came home early. At the Old Bailey Mr Stevenson asked her what happened.

Q. Was there any change in his mood or behaviour towards you?
A. Well, he seemed entirely different again. He was quite happy, and he was saying everything would be all right, we would soon have some money, and talking about marriage again and all kinds of other little things.
Q. Did he bring anything on that occasion?
A. Yes, he brought me the latest photograph he had had taken.
Q. Was that a recent photograph?
A. It was a photograph he had had taken. He was going to race a car – a 'Bristol' – at Le Mans this year, and he had to have a photograph taken, you see, and he had an enlargement which I had.

Q. He brought it to you, did he?

A. Yes.

Q. Did he write on it in your presence?

A. Yes – to Ruth with all my love, from David.

Q. Is that the photograph [a photograph is handed]?

A. Yes.

The Clerk of the Court: Exhibit 12, my Lord.

Q. My Lord, I wonder if she could sit down?

When she looked at the photograph Ruth cried.

Mr Justice Havers: Yes, certainly.

The Witness: No, it is quite all right.

Mr Justice Havers: Do, by all means.

The Witness: I do not want to sit down.

Mr Stevenson (to the witness): Did he stay in that evening and that night?

Q. How were you, the two of you?

A. We were very happy.

Q. Was there some discussion about how you could raise some money?

A. David said he was going to sell his racing car. I did not want him to.

Q. Why not?

A. Because he was so fond of motor racing. It seemed such a shame. He had built a car and then wanted to sell it. He said 'If you can find me £400 I won't need to sell it.'

Mr Stevenson then asked about the next night, Thursday. He did not deal with the events of the day, but they are interesting and relevant.

On Thursday morning Ruth was again enmeshed in jealousy and, as always, she phoned for her chauffeur.

Desmond arrived, and took her to Beaconsfield, a few miles from Penn, and like it full of two-car families, gracious living and smartened-up pubs. Desmond left Ruth in one of the pubs because the man who had taken the photograph that David had given her on the previous night had a shop in Beaconsfield. Ruth's object was to discover whether he had given this picture to any other woman. She never found the photographer and probably, after the first few gins, stayed in the pub. Desmond went to the 'Crown' at Penn to see what David was up to. He was there, but without the married woman. The two men did not speak; after the recent fight outside the Steering Wheel over the keys to Egerton Gardens, there was no pretence that they did not hate each other. David returned to work and Desmond drove back to Beaconsfield where he picked Ruth up.

What happened later was told at the Old Bailey.

Mr Stevenson: On Thursday, the 7th, had you booked seats for the theatre?

A. Yes.

Q. And he arrived in time for the theatre?

A. No, he phoned to say he was in a traffic jam, which was quite correct because he must have been phoning from a phone box somewhere on Western Avenue. I could hear cars and things. He was obviously stuck in a traffic jam.

Q. And did you, in fact, go to a film instead?

A. Yes.

Q. How were you getting on?

A. All through the cinema, which was rather annoying, he was telling me he loved me and all kinds of things – and a very good film. He seemed very attentive to me.

Q. And did you make – or did you discuss any plans on that occasion as to what you were going to do the following Easter weekend?

A. Yes, I understood we were going motor racing on the Monday.

Mr Stevenson: How were you going to spend the remainder of the Easter weekend?

A. We were going to take Andria out – we were going to take my son out. Mr Blakely was very fond of my son.

Q. Now on the morning of Good Friday, the 8th, did he leave in the morning?

A. Yes.

Q. What did he say he was going to do?

A. He left me about ten o'clock in the morning and said he was going to meet Anthony.

Q. Anthony Findlater?

A. Yes.

Q. On what sort of terms did you part on Good Friday morning?

A. On the very best of terms.

David did not give that impression to Ant and Carole Findlater, when he met them for a lunch time drink at the 'Magdala' public house. He was depressed and worried. Carole Findlater, recalling the meeting, thinks he must have had a row with Ruth before he left Egerton Gardens. If he had, Ruth did not mention it afterwards, but it was obviously in her interest to say that they had parted 'on the very of terms'. Equally, David had enough to make him despondent without the deflation of a row. He had clearly made an effort to be nice to Ruth by fussing over her at the cinema, a move that, judging from her evidence later, had irritated her – 'he was telling me he loved me and all kinds of things – and a very good film'. To him it probably seemed that as soon as Ruth thought she had got him back she was going to start her old game of making him do all the running. He must have been depressed about the car as well. His chances of raising the £400 for its repair were small and his appeal to Ruth the previous evening had probably been received with sympathy but no prospect of cash. Even Desmond would have hesitated to lend Ruth that amount to rebuild his rival's car, that important weapon in the love war.

Then there was Andy; no matter how fond David was of the boy, he cannot have welcomed the breakfast time atmosphere at No. 44 that Good Friday morning. David usually had a hangover and Andy was a very noisy boy of ten. Not only was he noisy, but he took little notice of his mother's orders because his mother had never taken much notice of him. He was proud of her, and always praised her beauty to his friends, but he disobeyed any command that did not please him. His favourite insult to his mother, which always annoyed her, was 'The cooking's bloody awful.'

To the nervous strain caused by Andy was added the black, crushing depression of sexual exhaustion. For months David had had to use drugs to satisfy Ruth's incessant demands for physical reassurance, and his own compulsion to find additional compensation with other women. Phials of Amyl Nitrite, a sexual stimulant, were in his pockets when the contents were listed at Hampstead Mortuary.

No wonder by the time the Findlaters met him at the 'Magdala', David was depressed. He told the Findlaters: 'I'm supposed to be calling for Ruth at eight tonight. I can't stand it any longer, I want to get away from her.'

There was nothing new about this sort of talk from David, indeed Ant particularly had heard it frequently and it had lost its novelty as pub time conversation. David then said: 'I daren't go back to Penn. If I do she'll come down there again.' Carole said: 'Don't be so bloody silly David, any man can leave any woman, what can she do about it?'

With unconscious prophecy David Blakely said: 'It's not as easy as all that. You don't know her, you don't know what she's capable of.'

Carole, who did not like Ruth, and thought David would be well rid of her, then did something that David appreciated: she made up his mind for him.

'Look, David, come back with us for lunch and stay the weekend, and if she causes any trouble we'll cope.' It seemed a reasonable arrangement between old friends; just helping a chum to avoid a too persistent mistress. After lunch David was still worried, but Carole repeated that there was nothing to fret over, they would deal with Ruth in a civilized, well-bred manner. David understood that this was a game two must play, he knew that Ruth's 'civilization' was Brixton, not Hampstead. He continued to look worried and fearful all that afternoon.

That morning Ruth had turned to Desmond Cussen, who was to her what the Findlaters were to David. She phoned him shortly after David left and Desmond picked her up and they returned with Andy to Goodwood Court for lunch. In the afternoon, they went to see a film about spacemen at the Plaza Cinema in the West End and around seven o'clock Desmond drove Ruth and her son back to Knightsbridge for Ruth to put Andy to bed. She was planning to get him settled before David returned to take her out for that drink with the Findlaters.

Desmond then went off to spend the evening with friends. In evidence at the Old Bailey neither Desmond nor Ruth referred to this time they had spent together.

When Ruth returned to Egerton Gardens, David and the Findlaters had already left Tanza Road for a drink; David did not want to go to the 'Magdala' in case Ruth appeared, and so they called at a pub in Highgate. Ruth waited at Egerton Gardens for David until about 9.30 pm and then rang Tanza Road; the phone was answered by the Findlaters' resident nanny for Francesca.

The nanny said that Mr and Mrs Findlater were not at home and she did not know whether Mr Blakely was with them, or not. She added that he was not in the flat at the moment.

By the time Ruth had phoned again, they had returned from the pub and Ant answered. She recounted the conversation at the Old Bailey.

Q. What did you say to him?
A. I said to him: 'Anthony, is David with you?'
Q. Yes?
A. And he said 'No.' So I said: 'I am very worried because he should have been back to meet me.'

The witness then repeated some evidence for Mr Justice Havers and continued:

I said: 'Do you think he is all right?' Mr Findlater replied and said: 'Oh, he is all right.'
Mr Stevenson (to the witness): Did he tell you where he was?
A. Yes, just before that he said that he had seen him earlier but that he had left.

Q. When you were told that he had left, did you believe it?
A. Not the way he said it. He said it rather cocky, as though, you know . . . well, I do not know quite how to say it.

During this conversation Ant, according to Ruth, laughed when he said 'Oh, he is all right.' She wrote, but did not say in evidence: 'I knew at once that David was there and that they were laughing at me behind my back.' That was something her vanity could not tolerate.

The reaction was as always: she phoned for Desmond, but he was not at home, so for the next hour or two she repeatedly dialled the Findlaters' number. Sometimes a voice would answer, and sometimes the phone was replaced when her voice was recognized. By the time Desmond had returned home and she had spoken to him it was midnight and at Tanza Road there was a rest from the phone calls. Carole decided to go to bed and took a sleeping pill to help her on what might be a difficult night. Before she went to bed she went into the sitting room where David was to sleep on a divan; he looked so scared and worried that she kissed him on the cheek saying: 'Don't worry, David, it will be all right, we all love you.'

Outside Ruth had arrived, spotted the parked Vanguard, and was very angry. Impatiently, she rang the Findlaters' door bell, but nobody came; after a time Ruth went to a call box and telephoned Ant. Someone hung up on her. She returned to pushing the door bell, nobody answered. In the early morning quiet of Tanza Road, she thought that she heard a woman giggle. In her state of baulked temper, she did not really know whether the giggle came from the Findlaters' flat or not. Mrs Findlater now thinks that it was unlikely to have been her and certainly not her nineteen-year-old nursemaid.

Ruth said at the Old Bailey: 'I was absolutely furious with David. I just wanted to see him and ask for the keys back . . . all kinds of things were going on. I just wanted him to jump in the lake, or go and lose himself, something silly.'

(The giggle inflamed her wounded pride.)

Q. What did you do next?

A. Well, my intention was to make a noise to make them come and open the front door. I was feeling just a little . . . in a peculiar mind then; rather a nasty mood to make them open the door, that was all.

Q. What did you in fact do?

A. Well, I knew the Vanguard windows were only stuck in with rubber, so I pushed at one of them and it came clean out from the rubber. It did not break it, just made a noise, and I did the same with two other windows. I did not break any, I just pushed them in. (Although she did not say so, Ruth used a rubber-coated torch from Desmond's car to help her.)

Ant came downstairs from the first floor flat and opened the door just enough for him to see and talk to Ruth who was on the doorstep; he was wearing pyjamas and a dressing gown. The time was about 2 am. When Ruth asked him 'Where is David, I want to speak to him?' Ant replied: 'I don't know where he is.' She said: 'I know where he is, ask him to come down.'

Summoned by Ant, and, unknown to Ruth, the police had arrived and were listening. The Inspector summed it up as another domestic tiff. Ant explained that the car belonged to a friend, that Ruth had damaged it, and would the police please send her home?

The Inspector examined the damage and quite calmly Ruth said that the car was 'just as much mine as his. I've been living with him for two years. I'm staying here until I see him. I'll pay for the damage.' Ant then said: Mr Blakely doesn't want to see her.' Ruth replied: 'I shall stay here all night until he has the guts to show his face.'

There was clearly no cause for the police to act, so the Inspector advised Ruth to go home and the patrol car drove off.

As Ruth did not go home but circled around the Vanguard, Ant again phoned for the police, who returned about 2.30 am, but Ruth had gone. She walked to the top of Tanza Road and Desmond took her back to Egerton Gardens.

At the trial Mr Stevenson asked her: 'What sort of night did you have?'

A. I did not go to sleep. I just smoked. I was still in a temper. I was very upset about the whole thing to think that David was behaving so disgustingly now. I was not well.

She wrote before her trial: 'I just could not believe, after all I had been through, that David could be such an unmitigated cad as to treat me as he had. If only I had been able to speak to him and give vent to my feelings, I do not think any of this would have happened. But I just could not get at him as he was shielding behind his friends . . . I knew then for certain that the Findlaters were trying to part us and I guessed that David would not have stayed unless there was some female attraction there. I knew him too well and I realized that it was probably the nineteen-year-old nursemaid.'

About half-past eight the next morning (Saturday), Ruth rang Tanza Road; as soon as she spoke the receiver at the other end went down. Seething, she returned to Hampstead and hid in a doorway a few houses away from No. 29. About ten o'clock Ant and David came out, looked up and down the street as they left the house, and as they did not see Ruth, came down the steps and examined the damage to the Vanguard's windows. After a short talk they drove off and Ruth guessed that they had gone to No. 12 Rex Place in Mayfair to repair the windows. Not only did Clive Gunnell work at Rex Place, but Ant also did odd jobs for the garage on demand. While they were repairing the car, Ruth telephoned. When Clive answered she said: 'I want to speak to Mr Findlater,' giving the name of another of David's girlfriends. When Ant answered she said: 'Thank you for calling the Black Maria last night. If I had known I would have waited for it.' Ant was too wary to reply. He had recognized Ruth's voice and he rang off.

Ruth then got Desmond to ring and ask for David; Desmond said that he was a Mr Lionel Leonard, a friend of David's. It was a Leonard MG that David had driven the previous summer in Holland. Ant again recognized the voice and before Desmond could say anything he hung up.

After Ruth's son Andy had been given lunch, he was provided with money and he went to the Zoo on his own. His mother was free to continue her man hunt. Desmond drove her to Hampstead about two o'clock and at the first place they looked, the 'Magdala' public house, they saw David's Vanguard parked outside with the windows repaired. Ruth decided that she would go back to Tanza Road before David left the pub, hide herself, and see who was in the party that returned to No. 29. She was no longer interested in seeing David and taking him home; that had been her policy on the previous night, and presumably that was her intention when she telephoned the garage earlier that morning. She was now convinced that David was having an affair with the nanny, whom she considered a desirable young bait provided by the Findlaters: a Machiavellian ploy to tempt David away from her. In fact although the nanny was young, she was a plump girl, not at all David's type. He liked fluffy blondes, preferably married and older than himself. Mrs Findlater knew David's weaknesses and if the 'bait' theory had been true would certainly not have tempted him with that nanny. The truth was, of course, that there was no 'plot', but Ruth could never accept that any man, let alone David, could possibly tire of her. She always thought that there was some plot or interference by others. Even drunken George Ellis would not have kept scuttling off to Warlingham Park if other wicked people, especially women, had not been telling him that he should leave Ruth.

A few doors away from the Findlaters' flat in Tanza Road – Ruth thought it was No. 33 – there were workmen going in and out. Ruth talked to some decorators in the ground floor flat and learned that it was for sale. Ruth pretended that she was interested, and the owner, who lived in the house, asked her to stay and have a cup of tea. Fortunately for Ruth they had tea in a drawing-room whose window gave a direct and clear view across the street to the front steps of No. 29.

As tea was served David and the party returned from the 'Magdala' and Ruth was disappointed that the nursemaid was not among them. About an hour later Mr and Mrs Findlater, accompanied by David and the nanny, who was carrying the baby, left the house and went off by car to the Vale of Health in Hampstead.

Ruth was then picked up by Desmond who had been

driving around looking for her, as he did not know of the strange tea party. On the way home she told him that she was convinced that David was having an affair with the new nanny. Ruth gave Andy, who had returned from the Zoo, some supper, and then she and Desmond drove again to Tanza Road, where she saw the Vanguard outside No. 29.

That evening, the Findlaters had asked a few friends round for a Saturday night drink. Among them was a psychologist called Charlotte, a woman with a compulsive giggle. Before the party had really got going, Charlotte had said to Carole after being introduced to David: 'Why does that young man look so worried?'

At her trial, Ruth aided by her Counsel Mr Melford Stevenson, gave a most disjointed and confused account of that Saturday night and early Sunday morning in Tanza Road. Mr Stevenson began by asking her what she saw.

Mrs Ellis: Obviously a party was taking place then.

Mr Justice Havers: Where were you this time?

A. Oh, just up the road. Just standing in the road.

Q. There was obviously a party going on in Mr Findlater's flat, is that what you say?

A. Yes, the window was open and there seemed to be a lot of noise coming from there.

Mr Stevenson: And voices were you able to hear?

A. Yes.

Q. Did you recognize any voice?

A. Yes, I heard David's voice.

Q. Any female voice?

A. Yes, I heard somebody giggling a lot. I had an idea it was somebody I knew, but . . .[Ruth never had a chance to finish. For some reason Mr Stevenson interrupted her].

Q. While you were watching there that evening, did you see any people come up to the house?

A. Yes, an open sports car pulled up and a man and a woman got out.

Q. Who were they?

A. I think it was Clive, but I would not be quite sure that it was.

Q. Clive would be Gunnell?

A. Yes.

Q. And with him a woman?

A. Yes.

Q. And how late did you remain watching that night?

A. It must have been about half-past nine or . . . half-past nine to ten, if not earlier, when David and Anthony came down the steps with a woman. I was standing by the side of Anthony's house.

Mr Justice Havers: David and?

A. David and a woman and Mr Findlater came down the steps of Mr Findlater's flat.

Mr Stevenson: Yes?

A. I was standing at the side of the flat. I heard David say . . .

Mr Justice Havers: Wait a minute . . . Yes?

A. I heard David say: 'Let me put my arm round you for support.' If they had turned round they would have seen me.

Q. Yes?

Mr Stevenson: Could you see who he was addressing when he said that?

A. I presumed it was the nanny, but I had never seen her before, except for a glimpse in the afternoon.

Q. How old was she roughly?

A. Young, I should think. She was dark, I know that.

Q. How long did you remain there that night?

A. Quite late. Twelve o'clock.

Q. What?

A. About 12.30.

Mr Justice Havers: I do not quite know what happened. Did they go off in the car?

A. They went off in the car, yes.

Mr Stevenson: You remained there until 12.30. Did you see them come back?

A. I went away and came back again.

Q. At what time did you come back?

A. When I came back, the cars were back again, so I gathered they had arrived back.

Q. You remained there until after midnight. Was the party still going on?

A. Yes.

Q. Again were you able to distinguish any voices?

A. Yes, the window was open.

Q. Whose voices could you hear?

A. I heard Anthony's and I heard David's, and I heard a woman giggling again.

Q. Did you know from earlier visits to the flat where the nanny slept?

A. Yes; Mrs Findlater had told me a couple of weeks before that the landlord of the flats or house was going to let her have one of his rooms, his front room, which they were doing up for the nanny.

Q. Was that above or below the Findlaters' flat?

A. Below – with a separate front door.

Q. As you were there, did you see anything happen?

A. Between 10 and 10.30 the nanny obviously had gone to her room, but the blinds were not down, and her light was on, and the light in the passage was on.

(Ruth had previously said it was about 9.30 to 10, if not earlier, when the nanny, David and Ant had left the house. She added that she had not seen them return. Then she agreed that she had left her post outside No. 29 at some unspecified time to return later. In her last reply she said that the nanny had obviously gone to her room between 10 and 10.30.)

Mr Stevenson: And then?

A. The party still continued, and the car that had driven up, the old sports car, was still outside, and I still heard the woman giggling. About 12.30 the blind in the nanny's room went down and the light in the hall went out.

Mr Justice Havers: The blind in the nanny's room went down and the light in the hall – what?

A. Went out as well and that was at 12.30.

Mr Stevenson: Were you able to hear Blakely's voice all the time?

A. After that, no, I could not hear it, although I listened for it.

Q. After when?

A. After 12.30 I could not hear it.

Mr Justice Havers: The lights were out everywhere?

A. No; the blind in the nanny's room had gone down and the light in the hall turned out.

Q. Was there a light anywhere else?

A. Yes; the party was still going on downstairs.

(As she had already said that the nanny's room was BELOW the Findlaters' flat the party had now somehow transferred to some unidentified part of the house.)

Mr Stevenson: The nanny had gone to bed and pulled down the blind, and at that time you no longer heard David's voice?

A. That is right. He could have been still there, but I did not hear his voice.

Q. The party downstairs [*sic*] was still going on, is that correct?

A. Yes.

Q. Rightly or wrongly, what did you think was happening?

A. I thought David was up to his tricks he was always doing.

Q. What sort of tricks?

A. Knowing David, I thought he might be having an affair with somebody else.

Q. With whom?

A. Perhaps the nanny might be the new attraction.

Q. Ultimately did you go home?

A. Yes.

Q. And again what sort of night did you have?

A. I did not sleep again.

Q. And what state of mind were you in?

A. I was very, very upset.

Before the trial Ruth had described her reactions to the nanny that night more clearly than she did in Court. She wrote: 'I remember thinking that it must have taken Carole a long time to think that one up. She wanted to get David away from me and she couldn't get him back herself so she did the next best thing. The Findlaters, who at that time had very little money, relied on David for their social life and I had been taking him away from them.'

There was no 'plot' concocted by Mrs Findlater over the nanny, and the idea that Carole and Ant were dependent on David for their social life was untrue. Carole had recently been appointed Woman's Editor of the *Daily Mail* and, although Ant's earnings were small, they were not short of money.

Equally mistaken was Ruth's sense of geography about the nanny's room. She did NOT sleep on the first floor, her bedroom was at the BACK of the house in the basement. The only way to reach this room was by going down the front steps and using the passage at the side of the house. The 'light in the front room' to which Ruth referred belonged to the landlord, not the nanny. The important thing is that on that Saturday night Ruth was convinced that he WAS having an affair; a conviction that buttressed her feeling that David, once again, had gone too far. During that week-end, Mrs Winstanley, the housekeeper at Egerton Gardens, noted that Ruth took down all the photographs of David that she had in the room and substituted pictures of herself taken while she was training at the modelling school. David was not the only one 'so much in love with himself'.

Early on Sunday morning Ruth returned to Egerton Gardens. This is what she claimed she did that Sunday. Later we shall see what really happened the day David died.

Her 'official' account was given at the trial.

Mr Stevenson: Ultimately did you go home?
A. Yes.
Q. And again what sort of night did you have?
A. I did not sleep again.
Q. And what state of mind were you in?
A. I was very, very upset.
Q. The next morning, which was the Easter Sunday, did you telephone the flat again?
A. Yes, I thought if David was sleeping in the lounge, and the divan is next to the phone, he would be the first to pick it up.
Q. Was it in the lounge he used to sleep when he went there?

A. Yes. There is no other room – only one bedroom and a small room.

Q. You telephoned?

A. Yes, just before 9.

Q. What happened?

A. What I thought would happen: the phone would either be answered by David, or picked up immediately and taken off to stop it from ringing. I waited a long time before it was answered and then Anthony answered the phone.

Q. That is Findlater?

A. Yes.


(Everyone was asleep when the phone rang, David was in the lounge, not in the nanny's room. By arrangement with Ant, David was not answering the phone, a job for which Ant had volunteered. It took Ant some time to wake up, get out of bed, and go to the lounge. Again the truth is unimportant. It was the effect of the misunderstanding on Ruth's jealousy at the time that was important.)


Mr Stevenson: What did you say?

A. I think I said: 'I hope you are having an enjoyable holiday, because you have ruined mine.'

Q. Did you remain in your flat until lunchtime?

A. Just before lunch, yes.

Q. What did you do then?

A. Mr Cussen picked me up with my son, and we went over, and I took something to eat at Mr Cussen's flat, and we spent some time in the flat.

Q. As far as the morning is concerned, were you waiting for a telephone call?

A. Yes, I thought David would still phone.

Q. And he did not?

A. No.

Q. How did you spend the afternoon?

A. I have completely forgotten what I did now. My son was with us, and we amused him in some way. I do not know what I did.

Q. At what time did you put the child to bed?

A. About 7.30.

Q. Was there still no message from Blakely?

A. No.

Mr Justice Havers: You had gone back to your flat by this time had you?

A. Yes.

Q. And what did you do next?

A. I put my son to bed.

Q. Yes. Go on.

A. I was very upset, and I had a peculiar idea I wanted to kill him.

Q. You had what?

A. I had an idea I wanted to kill him.

The object of this peculiar idea had spent the routine Sunday of any guest staying with young marrieds with a baby in Hampstead who had a nanny. At lunch time the Findlaters and David went to the 'Magdala' to meet Clive Gunnell and a friend. It was arranged that Clive should bring his record player to Tanza Road that evening and that David would collect Clive in the Vanguard from his home in nearby South Hill Park. That lunch time David cashed a cheque with the landlord for £5. In the afternoon, David and the Findlaters went up to Hampstead Heath and David, with Francesca on his shoulders, toured the fair.

When David drove to collect Clive and his gramophone, Carole went with him and the three had a drink at the 'Magdala'. The party to which they returned at No. 29 was small, alcoholically modest, with some beer and a little gin. Around 9 pm Carole had run out of cigarettes, and, a compulsive smoker, she appealed to David to 'pop down to the "Magdala" to get some'. Like a dutiful guest David went, and at the same time he suggested to Clive that they should also buy some more beer. These children of the non-walk society went in the Vanguard. Ruth arrived at Tanza Road, just after they had left, and not finding the Vanguard outside the house, also went to the pub. If the car had been outside No. 29 she would have hidden somewhere to see what happened, almost certainly out of effective .38 range. Anyone who has fired a .38 revolver knows that an amateur has to be very close indeed to hit even a large target.

Ruth Ellis did not miss; at the end of the chase, she was around the Vanguard, firing at David's back from a range of about three inches. To help her she was wearing her glasses. Although she was extremely short-sighted, Ruth normally did not wear her black-framed spectacles in public.

The post-mortem examination was made at 9.30 am on the next morning, Easter Monday, 11 April, by Dr Albert Charles Hunt, pathologist of the London Hospital Medical College. Inspector Davies and Detective Constable George Claiden were present.

At the Old Bailey, Mr Justice Havers in his summing up told the jury:

'You will remember that he [Dr Hunt] said there were four bullet wounds in the body . . . He said there was an entry wound of a bullet in the lower part of the back to the right and there was a track leading from this through the abdominal cavity perforating the intestine and liver and ending in an exit wound below the left shoulder blade and from this a track ran upwards through the chest perforating the left lung, the aorta, and the windpipe, and the bullet was lying in the deep muscles of the right of the tongue. He removed this bullet and handed it to Detective Constable Claiden later on. The next injury was just above the outer part of the left hip bone penetrating the skin and underlying fat only, and there was an exit wound quite close to that. He said there was also a shallow mark on the inner side of the left forearm. He could not be quite sure whether those last two injuries were caused by one bullet or by two. So that there was a minimum of three wounds, or possibly four. In the opinion of the doctor, the cause of death was shock and haemorrhage due to gunshot wounds.'

Mr Justice Havers, using the stilted tongue of the law, added: 'On that, Members of the Jury, I apprehend that you will feel constrained to come to the conclusion that this man died as the result of shock and haemorrhage due to the gunshot wounds caused by the bullets fired by the accused from that revolver.'

At 12.30 pm on the day of the post-mortem Inspector Davies saw Ruth at Hampstead Police Station. Again, when Davies told her that 'as a result of a post-mortem examination conducted on the body of David Blakely at Hampstead Mortuary this morning you will be charged with murdering him', she accepted the fact composedly. Davies cautioned her and she said 'I understand.' She was then charged, cautioned and the charge read over to her. She said: 'Thanks.'

At lunch time Ruth made a brief appearance at a special Bank Holiday Magistrates Court at Hampstead, and was then taken to Holloway Prison.

There was a brief reference to the court appearance on the BBC six o'clock news and some stories in the provincial papers. There was a national newspaper strike that kept this obviously sensational murder from most breakfast tables.

The strike ended a few days later but already teams of Fleet Street reporters were probing the backgrounds of the principal characters in the affair. It was not long before the first pornographic pictures of Ruth, taken in the back seat of a motor car, were trawled up. The trawlers agreed: 'Can't use that old boy, but bloody interesting background about the bird.' It was going to be a wonderful story for Fleet Street, the only worry the background researchers had was 'How much will come out in Court?' The answer, as it proved, was very little. Not much more appeared in the various 'background' pieces which were woven into the stories that appeared after Ruth's conviction. At the time few of those interviewed were prepared to tell what they knew.

The object of all this newspaper initiative was giving the authorities no trouble whatever at Holloway. She had asked for, and had been given, a photograph of David and a copy of the Bible.

On her first appearance in Court she had been granted a certificate of legal aid and a solicitor in Whetstone N20 was assigned to act for her. Later Mr John Bickford, then with Cardew-Smith & Ross, was instructed by a friend of Ruth's to act; after an interview at Holloway she decided to allow him to represent her. Mr Bickford was a solicitor of great experience. Pre-war he took part in the defence of Stoner in the notorious Stoner and Rattenbury murder. After the war he had been Public Prosecutor in the British Zone in Austria. He had also held high positions in the Colonial Legal Service.

# 7

# Holloway

Ruth spent the first days at Holloway reading, not the paperback gangster fiction that she normally liked, but the Bible. In prison this lapsed Roman Catholic returned to her faith. It was not the God of love and mercy that supported her, it was the Old Testament God of blood and vengeance; to those who visited her she said: 'An eye for an eye, a tooth for a tooth. I am quite happy to die.' At first she had not been quite sure that she would be hanged, and her friend Mrs Dyer recalled that Ruth's immediate question to her when she visited her in Holloway was: 'Are they going to hang me?' Before Mrs Dyer could answer this frontal probe Ruth went on: 'I don't mind, but go and see him and tell me what he looks like.' Mrs Dyer obeyed her friend's businesslike if unsettling instructions and discovered the body in an undertaker's in Sloane Street, a chapel of ease a few minutes away from Ruth's former room in Egerton Gardens. Mrs Dyer reported back that Mr Blakely was laid out in a white satin-lined coffin. Ruth was very pleased 'that he was being properly cared for'.

Two days after the shooting, probably on the same day that Mrs Dyer was receiving her instructions to find out where David was, Ruth wrote a letter to Mrs Cook.

Prisoner No. 9656 wrote:

'Dear Mrs Cook,

No doubt these last few days have been a shock to you.

Please try to believe me when I say, how deeply sorry I am to have caused you this unpleasantness.

No doubt you will hear all kinds of stories regarding David and I. Please do forgive him for decieving [sic] you, has [sic] regarding myself. David and I have spent many happy times together.

Thursday, 7 April, David arrived home at 7.15 p.m., he gave me the lastest photograph he had, a few days hence had taken, he told me he had given you one.

Friday morning at 10 o'clock he left and promised to return at 8 o'clock, but never did. The two people I blame for David's death, and my own, are the Finlayters [sic]. No doubt you will not understand this but *perhaps* before I hang you will know what I mean.

Please excuse my writing but the pen is shocking.

I implore you to try to forgive David for living with me, but we were very much in love with one another. Unfortunately David was not satisfied with one woman in his life.

I have forgiven David, I only wish I could have found it in my heart to have forgiven when he was alive.

Once again, I say I am very sorry to have caused you this misery and heartache.

I shall die loving your son, and you should feel content that his death has been repaid.

Goodbye,
Ruth Ellis.'

There is no real regret in this letter for what she had done. There are plenty of appeals to Mrs Cook to forgive her son but not once does her son's murderess ask for his mother's forgiveness. The self-centredness of it suggests madness.

An important point made in the letter is that Ruth had already decided that she was going to do her best to see that what she regarded as the 'guilt' of the Findlaters would be exposed.

Her constant complaint to those who visited her in prison was that it had been the 'interference' of others that had caused all the trouble; even now she would not accept that David had tired of her. It had been opportune that the Findlaters were willing to put David up and answer the telephone that Easter week-end, but their influence alone could never have made David decide not to return to Egerton Gardens. Ruth's delusion was shown when she wrote this from Holloway: 'My great mistake was when I went to live at Desmond's flat, that gave the Findlaters [this time she got the spelling right] a weapon with which to work on David and I am sure they were urging him to break with me. It accounts for all that business with the nanny – David had become so weak where women were concerned. He used not to be when I first met him, I think the fact that he was hard to get in the first place was part of his attraction to me when he originally started coming to the Little Club.' 'Hard to get' is, of course, a relative term, but Ruth's own admission that they were sleeping together within a fortnight of David coming to the club does not suggest that his resolution was strong.

To her family Ruth maintained the front of indifference to death. The loyal and still loving Desmond, who was a constant visitor, could not understand this composure. She refused to consider basing her defence at the Old Bailey on the very reasonable assumption that she was insane at the time of the shooting. There are two kinds of prisoners who plead insanity as justification – those who have committed crimes of such terrible ferocity or extent that they reason that any jury must accept their madness, and the truly mad whose insanity is obvious to even the most stubborn jury.

There is another class of prisoner who, although not certifiable, is deeply unbalanced, like James Hanratty, the petty thief, who became notorious when he shot and killed Michael Gregsten in a motor car on the A6. Hanratty then repeatedly shot Gregsten's girlfriend Valerie Storie to silence the only witness. Miss Storie lived, a cripple for life. Hanratty insisted that he was sane and would not allow insanity to be used as a defence. In his case there was a record of previous mental instability – a fact not mentioned in his defence when he was tried and convicted at Bedford Assizes.

Ruth's composure at Holloway was certainly partly induced by her study of the Bible and her belief that she would be at peace with God if she were executed. Another explanation is that, as always in her life, she was playing a part. When she appeared at the Old Bailey, she knew she would be a national figure. The fame that had unfairly passed her by so far was hers now. Ruth Ellis was not going to let Ruth Ellis down by any sign of weakness. To the world she would be the controlled, tough, brassy, and vaguely unlovable manageress of the Little Club. Her world was a hard place, she would maintain its tradition of not whining or squealing. She was sure, too, that when people heard how David had treated her and the way those wicked Findlaters had so successfully plotted to take him from her, they would all realize that she had been completely justified in shooting him.

Her 'toughness' was helped by her reading. One of the last paperbacks that she had consumed at Egerton Gardens was *Dead Reckoning*, an illustrated book of the film that had starred Humphrey Bogart, with Lizabeth Scott as 'Mike, a blonde femme fatale' the blurb said. In the book Mike shoots the wicked night club boss Martinelli 'and I saw Mike, standing by the car in her cape, still clutching her gun with both hands'.

Obviously Ruth did not read this book, with its clichés and phoney toughness, and then go out and murder David. This is just a small piece in the elaborate jig-saw of her mind.

In this age of motivation, psychiatry and Marx, there is a compulsion to explain away everything a human being does. Whatever the 'reasons' for Ruth's calmness and indifference it must never be overlooked that she was brave.

Ruth made another formal appearance at Hampstead Magistrates Court on 20 April and was remanded until 28 April. At this hearing the main police witnesses were called, among them Mr Desmond Cussen. Ruth Ellis was charged 'that on the 10 April 1955, at South Hill Park, Hampstead, in the County of London, she did murder David Moffett Drummond Blakely, Against the Peace of our Sovereign Lady the Queen, Her Crown and Dignity.'

The prisoner sat in the iron-railed dock, seldom looking at the over-full reporters' benches or at her friends and acquaintances who had come to see her on show, Among those present was Mr Morris Conley.

Ruth wore an off white tweed suit with black velvet piping. Her eyes had been made up, but although she was wearing a light lipstick she seemed to have no rouge on her cheeks. The pallor was enhanced by her platinum blonde hair. She was nervous, but there was no obvious deep anxiety in her face. She listened attentively as Mr J. Claxton began to establish the Crown's case. At this hearing she was represented by Mr Sebag Shaw, a most able and quick-thinking barrister.

Mr Claxton outlined the main facts of the story and made this comment about the situation, just before the shooting, at Egerton Gardens:

'What may appear to be a somewhat curious set of circumstances is that as soon as Blakely, who was known as Mr Ellis, left in the morning, Mr Cussen would come round and more often than not Mrs Ellis went out with him.'

In the dock Ruth looked annoyed, and it was clear that quite a lot of unflattering detail was going to emerge.

She was set-faced but calm when the gun was produced and P C. Thompson, the constable who had been having an off-duty drink in the 'Magdala' on the night of the shooting, demonstrated with it how Ruth had been found pointing the weapon at David as he lay on the pavement.

Even the appearance of Ant Findlater and Clive Gunnell as witnesses for the Crown produced only the occasional quick glance in their direction.

It was after lunch, when she had put on her black-framed spectacles and brought in a folded coat to cushion the hard wooden dock seat, that she was clearly upset by a witness. From her viewpoint, Desmond Cussen did not help her in his evidence.

From this pale man came the things she had so carefully omitted from her statement: the fact that she had had an affair with Cussen and Blakely at the same time in the summer of

1954; the story of how she had come to live at Goodwood Court, because 'she wanted to get rid of Blakely and not have him bothering her'; the money that Cussen had lent her; the chauffeuring Cussen had done to Tanza Road and how annoyed Ruth had been that anyone should dare call the police when she had banged in the windows of David's car.

As Desmond gave his evidence, she frequently tapped first one, then the other, of her black, high-heeled shoes against the iron railings of the dock.

It was nearly tea time when Desmond left the witness box and hurried out of the court without glancing at Ruth. He was the last witness for the Crown, and through Mr Sebag Shaw she pleaded not guilty to murder and reserved her defence; the magistrates committed her for trial at the Old Bailey.

The next morning's papers repaired the neglect imposed by the newspaper strike. *Daily Express* headlines read: 'Court hears of the loves of "Little Club" girl.' Witness says: 'She shot man on ground.' 'Race driver's friends tell of flat scene.'

The *Daily Mirror* said simply 'Model shot lover – court told'. 'She kept phoning.'

The *Daily Mail* ran a seven column screamer: 'Model shot car ace in the back.' 'Witness says her love had cooled.' 'Four bullets as he lay dying.'

On another page the *Mail* had a story headed: 'Director: My affair with Ruth Ellis.' (The director was Desmond.)

The vote on the Press table was that it was a bloody marvellous story and would be even better when it got to the Bailey.

There was one noteworthy incident that the reporters missed, but this was excusable as it occurred in the foyer of the court. It was the arrival, around 11 am, of George Ellis from Warrington, accompanied by Mr Tim Leuty, a reporter from the Manchester office of the *Sunday Pictorial*, the newspaper that had signed George up for his story, to be told when the case was no longer *sub judice* after the Old Bailey hearing. Wearing a camel hair coat and flapping his hands, Mr Ellis thundered into the hall. 'Stop the trial, stop the trial,' he ordered. 'I want to see my wife's lawyers.'

George Ellis was interviewed by a representative of Cardew-Smith & Ross in a nearby waiting-room. He soon realized that George was drunk so that to allow him through the closed door of the court would certainly not benefit their client, so he arranged for him to make a statement, later. Accompanied by Mr Leuty, George left quietly for the nearest pub. His subsequent statement was of small value and he was not called either by the defence or the prosecution at the Old Bailey.

The *Pictorial* never used his story, although one was prepared for him to sign. The reporter who had 'ghosted' this sent it to George for his approval but forgot to remove a confidential office memo which was clipped to it. The memo outlined George's depressing drunkenness and pointed out that George was then employed as Chief Dental Officer for Warrington at £1,850 a year. The memo said: 'I suggest we expose this bastard.' George was not pleased to read it, but the memo was not the reason why the *Pictorial* did not publish his story. George's solicitors had written to the editor of the paper and pointed out that publication, even though authorized by George, would ruin him professionally. The *Pictorial* spiked the story but used extracts when George committed suicide five years later.

Drunk, and unable to pay a hotel bill for £37, George strangled himself in a bedroom at Le Chalet at Corbière in

Jersey. He had lost his job at Warrington and in July 1958 had been convicted for drunkenness and a breach of the peace at Stockton Heath, Warrington. To the end he told anyone who would listen about Ruth: 'I was frightened to death of her. She was ruled by a passionate, uncontrolled, insane jealousy.'

In Holloway, Ruth was resolute that there should be no plea of insanity at the Old Bailey. Her brother Granville, in an interview published after her conviction, said: 'In Holloway she said to me, "Don't worry about me. There's nothing to be done. It's hopeless. I'm not worried and I've no regrets as to what lies ahead for me. The children are provided for and you are all right at home. I won't let them plead insanity for me. I'm not crazy, I know exactly what will happen. They are going to hang me."'

Her mother told the same story in her 'revelations' to Mr Godfrey Winn in the *Sunday Dispatch*: 'Ruth said to me over and over again, "It's no use, mother, I was sane when I did it, and I won't go to prison for ten years or more and come out old and finished. I'd much rather . . ."' The dots at the end of this statement were doubtless inserted by Mr Winn, or a drama-conscious sub-editor.

The prison medical authorities decided that she was fit to plead. Her electro-encephalograph recording showed no abnormality or epilepsy. Her health, too, apart from some sleeplessness, for which she was given drugs, was satisfactory.

In public Ruth was still the self-possessed and fearless blonde. That was how she seemed on 11 May when she made a three-minute appearance at the Old Bailey. Her Counsel, Mr Peter Rawlinson, told the Court that there were extensive inquiries still to be made and the trial was postponed to the next Sessions, beginning on 14 June 1955.

(Mr Rawlinson was one of the three counsel briefed to defend Ruth. The others were Mr Sebag Shaw and Mr Melford Stevenson, QC. Mr Stevenson was to lead.)

While Ruth was waiting to appear at the Old Bailey the psychiatrists were at work on both sides. The doctor retained by the Director of Public Prosecutions saw her on the afternoons of 9 and 10 June at Holloway. He found that Ruth was co-operative and did not evade any of his questions. She gave him no history of violent behaviour, uncontrolled outbursts of temper, or undue aggression. George Ellis was not consulted about her temper and David Blakely was unable to speak about his black eye and bruised back. Ruth told the psychiatrist that when she left her home on that Sunday evening she took with her a loaded gun with the intention of shooting Blakely.

She said that at the time she felt tired and run down; that she had a cold, and had had a two months' miscarriage some ten days previously, though this did not require any medical attention. She stated that after having shot David Blakely she felt no regret, and considered that she was justified in having done what she did because of the way in which he had treated her, and that she still felt so justified.

The psychiatrist felt that there was no evidence whatever that Mrs Ellis was suffering from any form of mental illness and that she had formed the intention of killing David some time beforehand and that she was aware of the possible consequences to herself of the act.

Dr Duncan Whittaker, MA, MRCS, LRCP, DPM, and Consultant in Psychological Medicine to the Woolwich & Bromley Group Management Committee, examined Mrs Ellis for two hours on Saturday, 4 June, on behalf of the defence, and much of his report was given in evidence at the Old Bailey. We shall consider it later, but there are two sections in this report which were not adequately dealt with at the trial. The first was:

'She indignantly denies that her behaviour of the week-end was hysterical, and said that on the whole she is a calm person. Nevertheless, her whole history is that of an emotionally immature person, and her present equanimity is "*la belle indifférence de l'hystérique*", whose intolerable problem has been solved at an immature level of behaviour and who is prepared to pay the price for this solution. Jealousy, of course, played a very large part, but it was her incapacity to get out of an intolerable situation which finally precipitated her action.'

The other observation was 'An emotionally mature woman would have been prevented from this action by thoughts of her children. I asked her about this point, and she told me that she never once thought of them.'

Ruth also stressed to Dr Whittaker that David had reduced her from being the successful manageress of her club to a neglected woman living in one room.

It is difficult for anyone, even a psychologist, to understand another person in a two-hour interview, but Dr Whittaker does seem to have grasped that damaged pride was a considerable element in the shooting. The Government psychiatrist also noted that Ruth still felt in Holloway that she was justified because of the way David had treated her.

# 8

## An Eye For An Eye

As the date for her appearance at the Old Bailey approached Ruth was able to ease the tension of waiting by concentrating, with her solicitor's assistance, on a vital issue: her hair was going very dark well above the roots and this, if not treated, would destroy the cool blonde image she wanted so much to show when she appeared in Court. At first the Governor of Holloway, Dr Charity Taylor, could find no rule whereby she might allow Ruth to have the materials needed for re-dyeing her hair, and it was not until three days before the trial that Dr Taylor's humanity sidestepped the Home Office and she permitted materials to be sent in. These had been prepared by Ruth's hairdresser, Shack's in Shaftesbury Avenue, together with a set of instructions. A wardress helped Ruth and when she appeared at Number One Court at the Central Criminal Court on Monday, 20 June, her hair was an impeccable Shaftesbury Avenue platinum blonde.

Shortly before she appeared in Court, her three counsel had gone to Holloway for a final conference with their client. Her basic desire was to have a chance to tell her story and show how the Findlaters had conspired to take David away from her. The Findlaters must be given the most searching cross-examination. Anthony Findlater had been called as a witness for the Crown. Mr Bickford, her solicitor, served a subpoena that week-end on Carole Findlater in case her evidence would be necessary for the defence. Mrs Ellis was delighted with the news. She went confidently to Court, not because she expected mercy, but because she was satisfied that the world would understand, if not condone, her action.

Number One Court, like many famous British institutions, is outwardly solid and not very impressive. The dominant feature is a great, sheathed sword of justice, bracketed to the wall above the Judge's chair which stands on a high dais at the far end of the Courtroom. When the Court is packed, as it was for the trial of Ruth Ellis, the atmosphere before the scarlet-robed judge enters from a door at the top right-hand corner of the room, is that of a small theatre on a first night. The barristers, solicitors and clerks in the well of the court are easing their tension in small talk. Above them is the tiny public gallery, predominantly jammed with those direct descendants of the patrons of the Roman Circus who have come not to see justice appear to be done, but to watch a fellow human being battle for life. Underneath the public gallery are the 'City Lands', a collection of green leather upholstered benches to which admission is by ticket only. Here, at an important trial, there is usually an audience of well-dressed men and women, some of whom may be the relatives of the barristers appearing in the case.

Opposite the judge to the rear of the court, is the vast wooden dock which is reached from the cells below by a tiled stairway. The jury box is empty, for those important ratepayers are empanelled later. Extra seats have been found for the Press, and the lucky ones have arrived in good time to ensure that nobody has filched their reserved places. Other reporters are there early to get the best possible view of the dock from the unreserved benches. The demand for Press seats has been extraordinary; in addition to the British reporters there are journalists from America, France, Italy and West Germany. Many of the foreigners cannot understand why the British may hang this woman for shooting her lover. From the whole Court there arises a controlled but almost musical pitch of excited talk. His Lordship and his officers in black knee breeches and white lace collars appear and the audience rises. Few cough, an indication of tense interest. His Lordship bows to the Court, the wigged heads of the barristers nod back, the audience resumes its seats and the star enters from the cells below. She is dressed in a black two-piece with a white blouse; her face is thinner than when she appeared at Hampstead in April but she smiles reassuringly at the blue-uniformed wardress who accompanies her into the box. Nobody will be able to say that Ruth Ellis is not playing her part competently. There is a quiet hum of chatter from the audience.

Everyone in the Court stops talking as the Clerk says: 'Ruth Ellis, you are charged that on the 10th of April last you murdered David Moffet Drummond Blakely. Are you guilty or not guilty?' The Prisoner: 'Not guilty.'

The tension eases away and everyone sits back while the jury are sworn, ten men and two women. Today is a big occasion, one that they will recall, they hope, in far-off bitter beer deliberations at the local. If the show is flat they will retire to consider their verdict deprived of a feeling of occasion and unwilling to argue long among themselves.

For a barrister this is one of the hardest theatres in the world to play. He must carry the jury with him emotionally and yet retain the respect of the judge for his legal arguments. In a murder trial where the accused is obviously guilty, he must above all try to raise enough sympathy for his client to ensure that the jury will consider a recommendation to mercy with their verdict. At the same time, he must not be so emotional that his Lordship tells him to stop talking drivel. His client must trust him and follow his lead, be reasonable in reply when necessary, and back him up when he is trying to appeal to a jury's instincts rather than their reason.

A barrister at Number One Court has to 'play the jury in'. They want time to get his measure. A murder jury likes and expects fireworks as part of the drama, but it needs a decent rest between rockets.

Mrs Ellis was represented by a strong assortment of barristers. Leading for her was Mr Melford Stevenson, QC, a distinguished-looking man, then aged fifty-two. His style, developed mainly in the less demanding atmosphere of the Divorce Court, was precise but not stimulating. He had had little experience of major criminal cases.

If either of her other barristers, Mr Sebag Shaw, then forty-eight, or Mr Peter Rawlinson, thirty-five, had led, the trial would have been a more flexible and spirited affair. The jury might have added a recommendation to mercy with their verdict. Mr Sebag Shaw, a man of splendid humanity, would certainly have made Ruth appear less of a blonde, mechanical doll in the witness box.

Undoubtedly her best advocate would have been Peter Rawlinson. He was a man with that indefinable Old Bailey touch. Young, good-looking, tall with fair hair, he had that attitude of well-mannered superiority that seven years of active service with the Brigade of Guards bestows. He knew exactly the sort of sensational point to make in cross-examination that delights a jury, experience he had gained in his defence of Alfred Charles Whiteway in the 1953 Teddington towpath murder. He knew, too, what excited public sympathy, for he had been attached to the legal department of Beaverbrook Newspapers.

The Crown was represented by Mr Christmas Humphreys, Mr Griffith Jones and Miss Southwood. Mr Humphreys, then fifty-four, was a civilized and gentle man with a very acute legal brain. He listed his recreations in *Who's Who* as: music, ballet, entertaining, Eastern philosophy and Chinese art. He was the Founding President of the Buddhist Lodge, London, and was the author of many books on the Buddhist religion. Nevertheless, he was a first-class performer at the Old Bailey, and few barristers could equal him in his 'feel' for the mood and atmosphere of a big murder trial. In 1955 he had been the Senior Prosecuting Counsel to the Crown at the Central Criminal Court for the last five years.

Mr Justice Hayers was not one of our most publicized judges, but he was a humane and decent man. Nobody can fault the way he conducted the trial and nobody could question the fairness of his summing up. He was sixty-five at the time of the trial.

In his opening address, Mr Humphreys gave the Court a moderate, reasoned, unshakeable case for the Crown, laced with enough spice and interest to command the jury's attention and to keep the news agency men and the evening newspaper reporters constantly on the telephone to their offices. It is only necessary to report parts of his speech.

'In a word the story which you are going to hear outlined is this, that in 1954 and 1955 she was having simultaneous love affairs with two men, one of whom was the deceased and the other a man called Cussen, whom I shall call before you.

'It would seem that Blakely, the deceased man, was trying to break off the connection. It would seem that the accused woman was angry at the thought that he should leave her, even although she had another lover at the time. She therefore took a gun which she knew to be fully loaded which she put in her bag. She says in a statement which she signed: "When I put the gun in my bag I intended to find David and shoot him." She found David and she shot him by emptying that revolver at him, four bullets going into his body, one hitting a bystander in the hand, and the sixth going we know not where.

'That in a very few words is the case for the Crown, and nothing else I say to you in however much detail will add to the stark simplicity of that story.'

He later added: 'But let me tell you at once, as no doubt his Lordship will echo, that you are not here in the least concerned with adultery or any sexual misconduct. You are not trying for immorality but for murder; and the only importance of these movements between her and these various men is that it will help you to see the frame of mind she was in when she did what it cannot be denied in fact she did.'

Then Mr Humphreys told how Mr Cussen, 'her alternative lover', had driven her up to Hampstead around midnight on Good Friday and how David refused to speak to her. 'Well by this time you have a fairly clear idea of the attitude of the man who was staying at the Findlaters' instead of spending the week-end with her.'

It was not a long address and he ended: 'Members of the Jury, there in its stark simplicity is the case for the Crown, and whatever be the background and whatever may have been in her mind up to the time when she took that gun, if you have no doubt that she took that gun with the sole purpose of finding and shooting David Blakely and that she then shot him dead, in my submission to you, subject to His Lordship's ruling in law, the only verdict is wilful murder. If during the trial any matters arise which enable you, under His Lordship's direction, to find some lesser verdict, then you will so do.

'Now with the assistance of my learned friends, I will call the evidence before you.'

Nobody could say that Mr Humphreys had been unfair; he had succeeded in what he had set out to do, establish Ruth as a rejected mistress who had shot her lover. He had also established that if love had played a part in the motive it was a strange love, an affection that was apparently shared between two men at the same time. It was not for Mr Humphreys to explain to the jury that to Ruth there was nothing inconsistent with occasionally allowing a man like Cussen, who lent and gave her money, to have sexual intercourse in return. This did not alter her conception of fidelity to David, the man she wanted to marry. When Mr Humphreys sat down, many members of the jury turned their heads to have a good look at this immoral killer. Mr Stevenson would have to work hard to change that image.

The first scene was over and the Court relaxed while Miss Southwood examined the minor witnesses for the Crown. Philip Banyard, Police Constable 161, 'S' Division, told how he prepared a plan of the area of the shooting. Mr Stevenson had no questions.

Thomas Macmacken, Detective Constable, Photographic Department, New Scotland Yard, told how he photographed David Blakely in the Hampstead Mortuary. Mr Stevenson had no questions.

Mrs Joan Ada Georgina Dayrell Winstanley, the house-keeper at Egerton Gardens, gave evidence that Ruth and David shared the same bed and that she knew him as Mr Ellis. Mr Stevenson had no questions.

Desmond Edward Cussen then went into the witness box. He looked anxious and his face was so pale that his black hair-line moustache stood out so clearly that it seemed to have been painted on. Mr Humphreys then examined Mr Cussen and established what he had already told the Court of the sexual relationship between Desmond and Ruth and of Desmond's part in the events of Good Friday at Tanza Road. It was a very short examination of a principal witness and ended like this:

Q. On Sunday the 10th of April did she and her son spend most of the day with you at your flat?
A. Yes.
Q. How old was the boy?
A. Ten.
Q. That evening did you drive her back to Egerton Gardens?
A. Yes.
Q. About what time?
A. About 7.30.
Q. At 7.30 on the Sunday night, and that is the last you saw of her?
A. Yes.

Mr Humphreys was no doubt asking these questions and those about the events of Good Friday against the time when he might cross-examine Mrs Ellis on her statement. He had already told the jury: 'The only comment I would make upon that statement . . . is that she never mentions Cussen from start to end.'

Mr Stevenson handled Cussen with circumspection in an extremely short cross-examination. It is reproduced here in full.

Q. You have told the jury that you and this young woman were lovers for a short time in June, 1954. Is that right?
A. Yes.

Q. And that was a time when Blakely was away, was it not – at the Le Mans race in France?

A. Yes.

Q. Were you very much in love with this young woman?

A. I was terribly fond of her at the time, yes.

Q. Did she tell you from time to time that she would like to get away from Blakely, but could not, or words to that effect?

A. Yes.

Q. And at that time did she repeatedly go back to him?

A. Yes.

Q. At a time when you were begging her to marry you if she could?

A. Yes.

Q. Have you ever seen any marks or bruises on her?

A. Yes.

Q. How often?

A. On several occasions.

Q. How recently before Easter had you seen marks of that kind?

A. On one occasion when I was taking her to a dance.

Q. When was that?

A. The 25th of February.

Mr Justice Havers: Of this year?

A. Yes, my Lord.

Q. 'When I was taking her to a dance?'

A. Yes.

Mr Melford Stevenson: Did you help to disguise bruises on her shoulders?

A. Yes.

Q. Were they bad bruises?

A. Yes, and they required quite heavy make-up, too.

Q. I do not want to press you for details, but how often have you seen that sort of mark on her?

A. It must be on half a dozen occasions.

Q. Did you on one occasion take her to the Middlesex Hospital?

A. Yes I did.

Q. Why was that?

A. She came back when she was staying at my flat, and when I arrived back I found her in a very bad condition.

Q. In what respect?

A. She had definitely been very badly bruised all over the body.

Q. Did she receive treatment for that condition at Middlesex Hospital?

A. Yes.

That was the end of the cross-examination. It did little to destroy the image of Ruth as a hard blonde living with two men at the same time, even if one, on Desmond's admission, was most willing to marry her. The jury had, however, been interested in the questions about the bruising. Neither Ruth nor Desmond appeared to look directly at each other during the hearing.

The next witness for the Crown was Mr Findlater, and Ruth watched him carefully as he took the oath. Mr Humphreys soon confirmed one of the main points in his address to the jury earlier that David had been trying to leave Ruth. He asked Ant about the incident when he and Clive went to Goodwood Court to rescue David.

Q. You went with Mr Gunnell and when you got there there was the accused and Blakely?

A. Yes, that is right.

Q. What was the substance of that conversation? What was it about?

A. He asked me if I could assist him to leave without Mrs Ellis.

Q. Was it in the accused's presence that he said this?

A. Yes.

Q. Could you help him to leave her?

A. Yes.

The examination was short and apart from establishing that David had wanted to leave Ruth, it dealt with the events of the Easter week-end, leading up to when David and Clive left Tanza Road for more beer.

Everyone was now waiting for Mr Stevenson to slow down the rapid speed at which the trial was moving. The jury and Ruth clearly expected a prolonged cross-examination of Ant. She was unaware that Mr Stevenson had apparently decided to submit Ant to the minmum of cross-examination, a decision no doubt made to avoid what he termed 'unnecessary mud-slinging'. The start was at least promising.

Q. You for some time received £10 a week, did you not, from Blakely for your services in connection with a racing motor car which he was building?

A. Yes, that is right.

Q. Was that at that time your sole source of income?

A. Yes it was.

No doubt Ruth thought there would be questions now involving Carole and David, the man who had supported her husband. Instead Mr Stevenson, out of the blue, asked Ant:

Q. When you saw Blakely and Mrs Ellis at the flat at Marylebone Road, had Blakely asked you to go there?

A. Yes.

Q. And asked you to go there because he wanted your help. Is that right?

A. Yes, he wanted my help.

Following his own form of logical sequence, Mr Stevenson switched his questioning to cover the telephone calls Ruth had made to Tanza Road on the Good Friday.

Ant admitted that he had lied when he said to Ruth that David was not there. Mr Stevenson temporarily abandoned the telephone line of questioning and asked:

Q. It was the night of Good Friday and Easter Saturday that she pushed in the windows of Blakely's car?

A. Yes, that is right.

Q. When I say 'pushed in' she put such pressure on them, or some of them, that they came out of their rubber seating. Is that right?

A. Yes, that is right.

Q. You know something about motor cars, I suppose?

A. Yes.

Q. Would it be right to say that in order to push such windows out of their rubber seatings you would have to exert great pressure?

A. Not a great pressure, I think. I think a good sort of thump, or something like that, would push them out. It is not great pressure.

Q. At any rate, how many windows did she push out that night?

A. One side one, and two back ones, I think.

Mr Stevenson, baffled over the windows, returned to questioning him about the telephoning.

Q. Was it quite plain when you spoke to her on the telephone that she was in a desperate state of emotion?

A. No.

Q. What?

A. I said no.

Q. Do you mean she was quite calm? Do you really mean that?

A. It was just a telephone conversation. She rang me up, as she had done hundreds of times, and asked if I knew where David was. It was just a telephone conversation.

Q. I know it was just a telephone conversation. Just bear in mind what she said and the way she said it and the fact that she afterwards pushed out those windows. Did you observe no indication of her being a very desperate woman at that time?

A. No.

Q. Never mind about the word 'desperate'. Was it obvious to you that she was in a state of considerable emotional disturbance?

A. Well, I did not get that impression over the phone. She might have been.

For the first time Mr Stevenson had got an admission out of Ant that perhaps Ruth was in an agitated state that night, but instead of hammering away at what was clearly a hostile witness, his next question was half-hearted and immediately parried by the very wide awake Ant. Mr Stevenson: Perhaps you are not very good at judging that sort of thing on the telephone. Are you?

A. I think so.

Mr Stevenson had no better luck with Ant over the young nanny who had been in the house that week-end. He could not establish that David had said to the nanny on Saturday evening walking down the steps of No. 29, 'Let me put my arm around you for support.' In any case the only question that Ruth wanted him to put was 'Did you and your wife deliberately dangle this attractive young woman in front of David with the idea that he should fall for her and so leave Mrs Ellis alone that week-end?'

The end of this truly miserable cross-examination came when Mr Stevenson, for no apparent reason, except possibly he had to finish somewhere, said: 'Your wife was in this flat all through the week-end, was not she?'

A. Yes.

It was left for Mr Humphreys in his re-examination of Ant to do part of Mr Stevenson's job. Perhaps Mr Humphreys felt Mrs Ellis was being unnecessarily deprived of legal assistance.

Mr Humphreys: You will appreciate what is being suggested, that there is some reason for Ruth Ellis being jealous by some reason of some new woman being on the stage.

A. I did not even know that Mrs Ellis knew we had a nanny. She knew we had one, but this was quite a new one.

Q. What my friend is putting is that Ruth Ellis in hanging about might have seen Blakely in the presence of an entirely new young woman. I am sure you will help us if you can, if you were fooling about or anything of that sort. Was there any incident with a young woman outside the house that you can remember?

A. No. (The witness withdrew.)

Now it was the turn of Bertram Clive Gunnell, and when he answered Mr Humphreys he confirmed that he and Ant went to Desmond's flat to take David away from Ruth. He also gave evidence which supported Mr Humphrey's earlier account, in his address, of the way in which David Blakely had been shot by Ruth. Mr Melford Stevenson had no questions.

Clive Gunnell was followed by Lewis Charles Nickolls, the Director of the Metropolitan Police Laboratories, New Scotland Yard, a brisk-speaking and highly confident expert witness. He gave evidence that the gun taken from Ruth outside the 'Magdala' was the one from which the bullets had been fired that killed David.

The most incisive part of his evidence was nursed by Mr Humphreys, with his beautiful sense of timing, to appear at the end of the examination.

Q. Can you help us at all as to the distance from the body at which any of the bullets had been fired in respect of the wounds found in the body?

A. Yes. I examined the clothing of the deceased man and I found that on the left shoulder at the back of the jacket there was a bullet hole. This had been fired at a distance of less than three inches. (The official transcript does not mention the controlled whistles that this evidence produced in Court.)

Q. Will you identify the garment? (Handed.)

A. Yes. (Same exhibited to Jury.)

Mr Justice Havers: Why do you say that?

A. That is because of the circle of powder fouling round the hole. The others are all fired from a distance.

Mr Justice Havers: A powder fouling?

A. Yes. There is a circular powder residue. All the other
   shots had been fired at a distance.
Mr Melford Stevenson: No questions.

Two more witnesses were examined for the Crown, one
was PC Thompson who had arrested Ruth outside the
'Magdala', and the other was Mrs Gladys Kensington Yule,
who was hit in the thumb by a bullet fired by Ruth as Mrs
Yule and her husband were *en route* for a Sunday night
drink. Mrs Yule said that Ruth had chased David round the
car after she had fired at him.

Again there were no questions for either witness from
Mr Stevenson.

The Crown's case rolled on at tremendous pace. Witnesses gave evidence that David had been dead when he
arrived in the ambulance at New End Hospital. Dr Albert
Charles Hunt told how the bullets had killed him, and
Detective Constable George Claiden told how he had taken
possession of the bullets that had been in the body.

No witness was questioned by Mr Stevenson.

Chief Inspector Leslie Davies was then examined by Mr
Humphreys and gave his evidence in the unhurried, super-
ficially precise fashion of the experienced police officer; the
jury noted carefully his remark that immediately after Ruth
had been cautioned, despite her statement that she was 'very
confused', to Inspector Davies she 'seemed very composed'.

Mr Stevenson had no questions for Inspector Davies. He
then began his opening address for the defence.

He made it clear that he had deliberately abstained from
trying to probe the accuracy, or the motives, of the principal witnesses for the prosecution.

Mr Stevenson said: 'It cannot often happen in this Court

that in a case of this importance, wrought with such deep significance for the accused, that the whole of the Prosecution's story which has been described as one of stark simplicity, as indeed it is, passes without any challenge or question from those who are concerned to advance the defence.'

He then indicated his line of defence:

'One of the ingredients in that offence [murder] is what lawyers call malice, and the law of England in its mercy provides that if a person finding themselves in the position in which this unhappy young woman now is, has been the subject of such emotional disturbance operating upon her mind so as for the time being to unseat her judgment, to inhibit and cut off those censors which ordinarily control our conduct, then it is open to you, the Jury who are charged with the dreadful duty of trying her, to say that the offence of which she is guilty is not the offence of murder, but the offence of manslaughter, and that, members of the Jury, is what we, on her behalf, ask you to do in this case.'

He said later: 'It is always an unpleasant thing to say anything disagreeable about someone who is dead, but I venture to think the story she will unfold to you can leave no doubt in your minds that he [Blakely] was a most unpleasant person.

'You may take the view that there is really no doubt that this young woman was driven by the sufferings she endured at the hands of this man to do what she did, but it so operated on her mind that her judgment for the time being unseated, her understanding was gone, and that malice, which is an essential ingredient in the offence of murder, was absent in this case . . .

'Members of the Jury, that will depend upon the view you take of this girl when you see her here in the witness box. You will observe that she is now a calm and undisturbed person. You have got to try to put yourselves in the situation in which she found herself during that Easter week-end, when this man, whom she needed as one of the fundamental requirements of her existence having, as you will hear, promised to spend that week-end with her, having, as you will hear, shortly before amended his conduct and behaved towards her in a way that gave her every hope for the future and bestowed on her all the marks of attention as before, went away and chose to consort during that week-end with these rather odd people in Hampstead, in whose flat he spent the whole week-end. It was in those circumstances and driven to a frenzy which for the time being unseated her understanding that she committed the crime about which you have heard this morning so many details . . .

'You will hear, and I am going to call a very eminent psychologist who will tell you . . . that the effect of jealousy upon that feminine mind can so work as to unseat the reason and can operate to a degree in which a male mind is quite incapable of operating.

'Now, members of the Jury, there are dozens and dozens of cases in which the courts have considered this matter which is called provocation. It always has to be considered on the facts which arise in the individual case, but never before, as far as I know, and as far as all the industry of those associated with me can reveal, has any court had to consider a case in which the Defence rely upon jealousy, and the state of mind in which a woman gets when a man to whom she is devoted behaved as this one did, as constituting this defence of provocation.'

Ruth walked with a high-heeled clicking from the dock to the witness box, and was sworn. Although outwardly calm, she was inwardly boiling. For her the whole case was over. The Findlaters had escaped. She could see no point in answering questions now and her dejection was obvious as she replied to Mr Stevenson. At times she was inaudible at the back of the court and even Mr Justice Havers had difficulty in hearing her evidence.

Neither her answers nor Mr Stevenson's questions made her early association with David in the least human. If only he had got her to say that she went to bed with David because he came from a better social class than herself and she wanted to see what it was like, it would at least have shown that the woman was human. He could have stressed that the first abortion she had was her attempt not to involve a young man of good family, who was engaged to be married, in an unpleasant dilemma which might provoke a damaging scandal. Instead all he got from Ruth were matter-of-fact answers which dealt with the abortion as casually as a woman might discuss whether she should have the green, or green-patterned, carpet in the front room.

She dealt with David's first proposal of marriage in the same offhand way.

Mr Stevenson: Do you remember one night when you were at the flat with him the question of marriage cropping up between you?

A. Yes, he asked me to marry him.

Mr Justice Havers: About when was that?

Mr Stevenson: About how soon after he returned from Le Mans?

A. I cannot remeber the exact date.

Q. Not the exact date. How many days or weeks?

A. Maybe a couple of weeks. It may have been more. I cannot really remember.

That was how a proposal of marriage from a man that Mr Stevenson had told the jury was 'one of her fundamental requirements' was presented to them.

The best that Mr Stevenson got from her about her passionate feelings for David was:

Q. What happened to your feelings for him from that time onwards?
A. He was a very likeable person and I got very attached to him.

Much of Ruth's evidence has already been given earlier and there is no value in repeating it. What I have tried to do earlier when that evidence has been quoted is to describe the humanity that these curt court answers concealed.

Ruth did not want too much of her early life and call-girl activities disclosed in court and it is understandable that she did not wish to reveal that Andria was illegitimate, but Mr Stevenson might have done better to have thrown everything at the jury, good or bad. Then at least Ruth would have emerged as a person, not a mechanical, unfeeling doll.

Again and again Mr Stevenson threw away points where, with a little more skill, he could have won the jury's sympathy. He was not short of background information, for his brief, prepared by Ruth's solicitor after months of exacting effort, gave him all he needed. He appeared to have decided that it was best not to probe the unconventional, half-drunk world of Ruth Ellis, or to get behind the 'hostess front' and release to the Court the self-love, jealousy and ambition that was really her.

No jury, or anyone else, likes to hear of a woman being beaten by a man. Mr Stevenson made his first reference to David's violence just before the Court adjourned for lunch.

Q. How did the violence manifest itself?

A. He only used to hit me with his fists and hands, but I bruise very easily, and I was full of bruises on many occasions.

After lunch the frame of Mr Stevenson's examination remained unchanged, and there was no indication of the explosive relationship that had existed between Ruth and David.

Consider the account of one of the key situations – the moment when Ruth left the Little Club to live with Desmond at Goodwood Court, a move which had in Ruth's opinion been the biggest mistake she had made.

Mr Stevenson: And where did you go?

A. I moved to Mr Desmond Cussen's flat, Goodwood Court, Devonshire Street.

Q. And what was Blakely's attitude to your doing that?

A. He did not like me going to live with Desmond at the flat.

It went on without the least trace of human drama, and those wild chases to Penn and the midnight trips to Gower Street were reduced to emotional nothings.

Q. I do not want you to mention any names . . . but was there some trouble about a young woman.

A. Yes.

Q. And again without mentioning names was that woman down at Penn, or Beaconsfield?

A. In Penn.

Q. And did you on one occasion remain all night outside the house where that other woman was living?

A. Yes.

Q. And did you see Blakely come out in the morning?

A. He came out at nine o'clock in the morning. He had hidden his car at the back of the 'Crown' public house, which is just down the road.

Q. What were your feelings at that time?

A. I was obviously jealous of him now. I mean the tables had been turned. I was jealous of him, whereas he, before, had been jealous of me. I had now given up my business—what he had wanted me to do—left all my friends behind connected with clubs and things, and it was my turn to be jealous of him.

Ruth's account of her vigil outside Tanza Road when she thought David was having an affair with the nanny never really stirred the jury. They seemed uneasy at the speed at which the trial was moving. Mr Stevenson asked her:

Q. Rightly or wrongly, what did you think was happening?

A. I thought David was up to his tricks he was always doing.

Q. What sort of tricks?

A. Knowing David, I thought he might be having an affair with somebody else.

Q. With whom?

A. Perhaps the nanny might be the new attraction.

For a barrister who was trying to base his defence on the grounds that jealousy had unseated his client's reason, Mr Stevenson might have been expected to build up the effect of this 'affair' on his client's jealousy. Instead he said: 'Ultimately did you go home?' Ruth answered: 'Yes.'

Swiftly he led Ruth to describe how she set off the next day to shoot David. She did not mention jealousy once and the evidence was finished with these words:

Mr Stevenson: When you say that you had a peculiar idea that you wanted to kill him, were you able to control it?

A. No.

Q. And you went up and you in fact shot him? Is that right?

A. Yes.

Mr Stevenson sat down and Mr Humphreys got up. He had, with his experience of Number One Court, the exact feeling of the prisoner's mood; one of absolute depression and indifference, tinged with resentment. He knew that essentially Ruth had told the truth and that she would continue to answer direct questions in a straightforward manner no matter how incriminating the reply.

He moved unhesitatingly for the finale.

Q. Mrs Ellis, when you fired that revolver at close range into the body of David Blakely, what did you intend to do?

A. It was obvious that when I shot him I intended to kill him.

Mr Humphreys sat down. The Court seemed not to have understood what had happened. In the silence all eyes stared as the high heels clicked their way back from the witness box to the dock. It must have been the shortest cross-examination in a murder trial in the records of Number One Court. Mr Stevenson looked around the Court. He had the expression of a man who has been unexpectedly let down by a friend.

The next witness was Dr Duncan Whittaker, a rather unprepossessing man who told Mr Stevenson that he was a Master of Arts, a member of the Royal College of Surgeons and a licentiate of the Royal College of Physicians, and the holder of a diploma in Psychological Medicine. Neither the judge nor the jury seemed impressed by the first appearance of Dr Whittaker, nor did his qualifications dazzle them. British courts, especially in murder cases, are very wary about evidence from this kind of medical expert.

Dr Whittaker quoted Professor C.G. Jung to support his statement that 'women cannot so easily as men separate their sexual experiences with men from their total personal relationships'. To get Dr Whittaker out of this strange homosexual tangle Mr Stevenson translated this as 'a man's love is a man's boast, a woman's is her existence'.

Dr Whittaker was a difficult witness to pin down, as this exchange with Mr Stevenson shows.

Dr Whittaker: They are more prone to hysterical reactions than men.

Q. And under the influence of these hysterical reactions what becomes of their standards of conduct and control?

A. They are inclined to lose some of their inhibitory capacity and solve their problems on a more primitive level. This is not applying to women in general, but it is if they do have hysterical reactions they are more prone to hysterical reactions than men.

Mr Justice Havers bore patiently with Dr Whittaker until he introduced the argument that a person in the firing line in a war sometimes gets a paralysis that ensures his removal from the front. Mr Justice Havers said testily:

'I thought we were talking about women. What has the firing line got to do with a woman? If you want to talk about men, very well, but I thought we were talking about this woman.'

Up to this point Mr Stevenson appears to have been trying

to establish that hysterical women often do uncontrollable things. Unfortunately even this argument was destroyed when Dr Whittaker told the Court of his impression of Ruth when he interviewed her in Holloway:

'The feature which impressed me most was her equanimity. She had drifted into a situation which was for her intolerable, but she could find no way out, and she had not a sufficiently hysterical personality to solve her problems by a complete loss of memory.'

Q. Were you able to form any view as to her state of mind on the day she shot this man?
A. She was very disturbed.
Q. Yes. What else?
Mr Justice Havers: Are you talking about the day of the shooting, or the day you saw her?
A. The day of the shooting. She was not disturbed when I saw her. I think her mind was very definitely disturbed on that day.
Q. In what way?
A. The situation was now absolutely intolerable for her. She considered that he was being unfaithful at that moment, but she was convinced that he would return and she would not be able to resist him.
Mr Stevenson: Were you able to form any view about the subject of jealousy?
A. Yes, at that time she both hated and loved him; she had ambivalent emotions.
Q. When you get that duality of emotion, what does that indicate, so far as the patient is concerned?
A. Some degree of emotional immaturity – not intellectual, but emotional.

Mr Justice Havers: She had some degree of emotional immaturity?

A. Yes.

Mr Stevenson: Did you ask her any questions with a view to finding out whether she considered the consequences of what she was doing?

A. I asked her if she thought about her children. She said she did not think about them at all.

What Dr Whittaker had said in his report commissioned by the Defence was that 'an emotionally mature woman would have been prevented from this action by thoughts of her children'. If he had said this in Court, it would certainly have made Ruth more human and not reinforced, as his answer to Mr Stevenson did, the image of the cold bitch who never once thought of her children.

Mr Stevenson's next question did return to the question of his client's emotional immaturity.

Q. Having regard to the fact that she is, as you say, emotionally immature, and also to the effect that jealousy has the effect that you have indicated on a woman, and bearing in mind your own examination of Mrs Ellis, what view have you formed about this occurrence on Easter Sunday?

A. I have formed the view that if he had given her the chance to blow him up on the telephone the emotional tension would have been released, and the incident would not have occurred.

(As an explanation this reply ignored that on at least three occasions over that week-end, Ruth had a chance to speak to David, either in the street or in the 'Magdala'. She could

also have spoken to him and let off her emotional steam a
few moments before she fired the revolver.)

Dr Whittaker was then cross-examined by Mr Humphreys, who demolished him swiftly and skilfully.

Q. Dr Whittaker, do you regard her as being somewhat
   emotionally immature?
A. Yes.
Q. From the psychological point of view something of a
   hysteric?
A. Yes, but not a gross hysteric.
Q. In your view there was such emotional tension over the
   week-end without relief that she was impelled to resort
   to violent action to release that suppressed emotion?
A. Yes.
Q. In your view, at the time of the killing, she was mentally
   capable of forming the intent to kill?
A. Yes.
Q. In your view, was she at the time, within the meaning
   of the English law, sane or insane?
A. Sane.

After a few more questions the witness withdrew and Mr
Stevenson stood up and said: 'That is my case, my Lord.'

Mr Justice Havers then dismissed the jury so that Mr
Stevenson could convince him that he understood the law
in relation to provocation.

To reduce the charge of murder to one of manslaughter,
which was his declared objective, Mr Stevenson had to
prove that Ruth had been so provoked by some conduct on
the part of David that judge and jury would consider that
she could not help shooting him.

Mr Justice Havers asked Mr Stevenson: 'What do you say is the evidence of conduct on the part of this deceased man of a nature which has hitherto been considered by the Court to amount to provocation?'

Mr Stevenson said he could find no precedent either in this country or America that any court had 'ever considered the effect on the female mind of infidelity either in a spouse or a lover'.

Finally he took his stand on the basis that David's actions had provoked Ruth to such a state of jealousy that she lost control.

There were long exchanges between Mr Stevenson and Mr Justice Havers where Counsel tried to find some justification for what the judge described as 'new law'. None could be found. Mr Justice Havers remarked: 'That is very curious after all these years, because jealousy is one of the commonest emotions.'

He then asked Mr Stevenson another plain question: 'Does your proposition come to this, putting it in its simplest form: if a man associates with a woman, and he then leaves her suddenly, and does not communicate with her, and she is a jealous woman, emotionally disturbed, and goes out and shoots him, that is sufficient ground for the jury to reduce the crime of murder to manslaughter?'

Mr Stevenson could not, obviously, give a direct answer. He knew that Mr Justice Havers was right. In English law there is nothing which admits the defence of *crime passionnel*.

Mr Stevenson could not answer Mr Justice Havers's last question.

Mr Christmas Humphreys then gave his view of Mr Stevenson's attempt to create new law. He said: 'I accept my learned friend's proposition that this woman was disgracefully treated by the man who died, and I accept my learned friend's proposition that it would tend to lead her into an intensely emotional condition even as that hypothetical person "the ordinary reasonable human being" . . . but was she brought more than into a state where it would be reasonable for her to hit and hurt him? One must take into consideration that the actual crime was planned – prepared; there was some pursuit of that purpose through the streets of London [presumably Mr Humphreys was referring to Ruth's account of how she took a taxi from Egerton Gardens to Tanza Road] and the time of an hour or two, and finally, the man she killed was an unarmed man, and without any semblance of a struggle she shot him in the back.'

The Court adjourned until Tuesday 21 June at 10.30 am.

In the morning Mr Justice Havers addressed the Court before the jury were re-admitted. He said: 'I feel constrained to rule that there is not sufficient material even on a view of the evidence most favourable to the accused for a reasonable jury to form the view that a reasonable person so provoked could be driven, through transport of passion and loss of self-control, to the degree and method and continuance of violence which produces the death, and consequently it is my duty as a judge, and as a matter of law, to direct the jury that the evidence in this case does not support a verdict of manslaughter on the grounds of provocation.'

In the dock Ruth sat unmoved by this warning that she must be sentenced to death.

Mr Stevenson accepted the defeat without question. He also agreed that it would now be improper for him to address the jury again. Any chance that his final address might change the picture he had allowed the jury to get of his client, vanished. To those ten men and two women the issue was easy. This hard-faced, unemotional woman had been left by a man and because she was jealous, she had shot him in the back, one shot having been fired from a distance of less than three inches. Any reasonable body of English ratepayers, especially one where the men out-number the women by five to one, was certainly not going to take a lenient view of that sort of foreign habit.

Mr Justice Havers then summed up. Obviously he stressed that matter of the three inches, but his summary of the evidence was logical and dispassionate. The kernel of his speech was this: 'I apprehend that you will have no difficulty in coming to the conclusion that it was the accused who fired six shots from that revolver at Mr David Blakely. If you are satisfied about that, the other question you have got to determine is whether the prosecution has satisfied you that at the same time she fired those shots she had an intention to kill or to do grievous bodily harm.'

The jury only had to remember Ruth's answer to the one question Mr Humphreys had asked her – 'It is obvious that when I shot him I intended to kill him.'

Mr Justice Havers then told them what he had already told Mr Stevenson and Mr Humphreys that it was 'not, even on a view of the evidence most favourable to the defendant' possible to bring in a verdict of manslaughter.

'Even', he said, 'if you accept every word of it [her evidence] it does not seem to me to establish any sort of defence to the charge of murder.'

Later he said: 'According to our law, members of the jury, it is no defence for a woman who is charged with the murder of her lover to prove that she was a jealous woman and had been badly treated by her lover and was in ill-health and, after her lover promised to spend the Easter holidays with

her, he left her without any warning and refused to communicate with her, or that he spent holidays with his friend, or
in the company of another woman, or if he was committing
misconduct with another woman, and that as a result of that
she became furious with him and emotionally upset and
formed an intention to kill him which she could not control.
None of these facts individually afford any defence, nor do
they collectively afford any defence.'

The jury retired at 11.52 am. Obviously the Court officials thought that they would spend some considerable time
over their verdict, for the jury was sworn for another case.
The fashionable ladies of the City Lands settled down to
pass the time. The clerk read out the charge of buggery.
Those who had come to hear a murder case showed on
their faces that they did not care for this at all.

Fortunately they were spared any details as Ruth's jury
sent a message that they were returning. The accused man
was taken downstairs and Ruth was brought up to hear the
verdict. The jury had been absent fourteen minutes, just
long enough for a very brief discussion. There could have
been no discussion about a recommendation to mercy.

When the foreman gave his verdict of 'Guilty', he
observed the convention of Number One Court and did
not look at the accused. She accepted it, as conventionally
as the foreman gave it, with outward calm, and after the
ritual of the sentence of death by hanging in a lawful place
of execution was over, she turned about, and with a smile
for her parents and friends in the back of the court, clicked
briskly down the stairs to the cells. Nobody could say that
Ruth Ellis had not played her part as well as any Hollywood
gangster's moll sent to fry by the District Attorney.

# 9

# The Gun

The drama was over and the set routine of the last three weeks in the life of a convicted murderer began. Ruth saw her father and solicitor before she left the Old Bailey for the death cell at Holloway. There she would be watched and observed by day and by night until she walked to the execution shed that adjoins the cell. The hanging was to be on 13 July. Even the death cell did not disturb her outward composure and after visiting Ruth the day following her conviction, her solicitor announced that there would be no appeal. Apart from Ruth's wish not to appeal, this was a sensible decision legally. There were no grounds on which she could appeal and such a move would have irritated the authorities. In them, and especially the Home Secretary Major Gwilym Lloyd-George, was her last hope of life. Obviously her solicitor Mr Bickford was encouraged by what Mr Christmas Humphreys had said at the trial when he admitted that Ruth had been disgracefully treated by David and that this would tend to lead her into an intensely emotional state. He added: 'I agree, of course, that all these considerations may well apply in some other place.' Mr Bickford immediately began collecting material in support of a plea for reprieve; he did this on his own initiative, for immediately after the trial Ruth was indifferent about an appeal for mercy.

To her parents she maintained her philosophy of an eye for an eye, and told her mother that she did not want her to organize a petition for reprieve. Her routine in the death cell was calm and uncomplicated. She made dolls from the materials brought her by Mrs Neilson, she did jig-saw puzzles, and she continued to read the Bible. There was an hour's exercise a day and a ration of cigarettes. Ruth did not drink the beer available to the condemned. News of this extraordinary calm was soon known to the public, who puzzled how any human being so near to death could behave in such an inhuman way.

If the atmosphere inside Holloway was calm the mood outside was disturbed. The abolitionists were active; there were letters to the newspapers from Sir Beverley Baxter and Mr Anthony Greenwood, MP, and the Methodist leader Dr Donald Soper said that he did not think Ruth Ellis should hang. Petitions were organized and the sponsors claimed that they collected 50,000 signatures for a reprieve. Mr Sidney Silverman, MP, wrote with more feeling than accuracy in the *Star*. 'She is certainly not accustomed to violence or to crime. She is not a twisted pervert obtaining strange satisfaction by nameless abnormalities.'

The abolitionists had a wonderful propaganda vehicle in Ruth Ellis; she was young, pretty, and the mother of two children; and naturally they made the most of it. However, a few months previously there had been no such outburst over the hanging of Mrs Styllou Christofi, who had strangled her daughter-in-law and then set fire to the body in a Hampstead back garden. There was no great public concern in the case, as Mrs Christofi was fifty-one, ugly, and she was also a Cypriot who spoke poor English.

Public interest in Ruth Ellis was kept bubbling by the newspapers. In the *Woman's Sunday Mirror* Mrs Ellis told her own story. In the *Sunday Dispatch* there were the reminiscences of her mother, as told to Mr Godfrey Winn. The *Empire News* had the offerings of Mrs Jackie Dyer, the young French-born woman who had been Ruth's barmaid at the Little Club. In addition, Ruth's brother Granville was to hand for interviews in the *Empire News* and the *Sunday Graphic*. Another brother, Arthur, suddenly appeared to join in the general press excitement. He was interviewed by the *Woman's Sunday Mirror*.

The most moving argument for the abolitionists came from Mr William Connor who wrote, under his pen-name of 'Cassandra', in the *Daily Mirror* on 30 June 1955: 'Ruth Ellis does not matter any more than her two most recent female predecessors to the hangman's noose – Mrs Merrifield and Mrs Christofi.

'But what we do to her – you and I – matters very much, and if we continue to do it to her sad successors then we all bear the guilt of savagery untinged with mercy.'

The hangers had an eloquent witness in Mrs Gladys Yule, who had been shot in the thumb by one of Ruth's stray bullets while sauntering down to the 'Magdala' with her husband for a Sunday night drink. She wrote in the *Evening Standard*: 'Don't let us turn Ruth Ellis into a national heroine. I stood petrified and watched her kill David Blakely in cold blood, even putting two further bullets into him as he lay bleeding to death on the ground.

'What right had Ruth Ellis to be jealous of Blakely, jealous to the point of killing, even if there had been "another woman"? . . . These hysterical people, getting up petitions for a reprieve and then rushing to sign them. Do they realize that Ruth Ellis shot David Blakely to the danger of the public?

'She might easily have killed me as an innocent passer-by,

a complete stranger. As it is I have a partly crippled right hand for life for which there is no compensation.

'If Ruth Ellis is reprieved we may have other vindictive and jealous young women shooting their boy friends in public and probably innocent blood on their hands.

'*Crime passionnel* indeed! What if other countries would let her off from her just punishment? When has Britain followed the lead of others?

'Let us remain a law-abiding country where citizens can live and walk abroad in peace and safety.'

As Mrs Yule pointed out in her letter, foreigners, through their newspapers, were critical of the 'barbaric British', an indignation that ran down from Scandinavia through West Germany to France. Even the Americans, to whom murder is a small novelty, were intrigued by this cold, calm woman in Holloway.

Ruth herself after a week in the death cell was beginning to recover from the shock and excitement of the Old Bailey. She began to lose confidence in John Bickford and started to criticise him bitterly for failing to put Carole Findlater in the box at her trial. After she had been sentenced Bickford immediately went to see her in the cells at the Old Bailey. He said afterwards that she was calm but tearful but that she complained bitterly: 'I don't mind dying but I don't see why they should get away with it.' She was, as Bickford later told me, referring to the Findlaters.

It was useless Bickford trying to explain that he had done his best; he had served Carole with a subpoena, but on the morning of the trial Melford Stevenson had decided not to call Carole. He told Bickford that he could not see how it would help Ruth to reveal that Carole had once left her husband to live with David for several months before returning to Ant. An integral part of Ruth's defence was that the Find-laters were dangling the nanny as sexual bait for David, not that he was still having an affair with Carole.

For his part Bickford tried to calm Ruth's bitterness by stressing that she had an excellent chance of a reprieve. Whatever effect this had on Ruth was not evident to those who visited her. To her mother and father and to Jackie Dyer, she insisted she was still prepared to die – an eye for an eye was still her credo. Mrs Dyer, however, would not accept Ruth's death wish. She sought the help of Mr George Rogers, the Labour MP for North Kensington, where she lived. Mrs Dyer hoped George Rogers would persuade Ruth to confess that Desmond Cussen had given her a gun and persuaded her to shoot David, his love rival.

On 29 June Mr Rogers met Ruth at Holloway. After-wards he reported: 'She was a poor little pale thing in a grey dress. She wore no make-up and her hair was done in a pony tail style.' He wrote to the Home Secretary and urged him to reprieve Ruth. Major Lloyd-George acknowledged the letter but did not ask Mr Rogers to discuss the case with him. Perhaps Lloyd-George was influenced by reports from Holloway detailing Mr Rogers' behaviour when he visited Ruth Ellis. The day after the visit the Governor of Hollo-way, Dr Charity Taylor, wrote angrily to the Home Secretary, copying her letter to the Prison Commissioners:

I beg to state for your information that at approximately 7.10 p.m., on the 29th June I paid a routine visit to Ruth Ellis in the condemned cell. She told me that the MP I had told her of during the morning had been to see her. She said he was a great talker and she was too tired to argue with him. She said that she had agreed with him that there were matters she had not disclosed, but she did not want to as she did not want more scandal. She told me she hoped he would fail in his efforts and she would pray that he did.

I have never seen Ruth Ellis so distressed, and the Officers reported that for the first time she had cried. She told me she supposed it was too late to change her mind as he was going to the Home Secretary in the morning.

I did not ask her, but I formed a strong impression that she did not wish Mr Rogers to pursue the subject of a reprieve.

When I visited the Centre of the Prison, Principal Officer Griffin reported that she had taken the visit with Ellis and Mr Rogers and that he had 'badgered' her. Miss Griffin's statement is attached . . .

Principal Officer Griffin's report stated that:

[Rogers] introduced himself, then said that all her friends and relatives were distressed at her position, in particular J. Dyer had approached him and asked him to do all he could for her. He kept on to her about living for her child's sake, her attitude in wanting to die was all wrong, did she believe in the After World, she needn't think that by her dying she would be with David Blakeley [sic]. She should live and expedite (? expiate) her crime on earth. Would she give him authority to approach the Home Secretary for clemency. Did she believe in God, because if she did, she should have the will to live.

Ellis, in reply said she did not want to live and that her child was being taken proper care of. She has no wish or desire to live.

Mr Rodgers [sic] was so persistent that Ellis very

grudgingly said, What if you do ask for Clemency and it fails, I shall still be in the same place. Mr Rodgers's reply was 'I never fail'. Mr Rodgers said she hadn't told them about when she got the gun. Ellis told him that Mr Bickford had all the information necessary. Mr Rodgers then told her to pray and think about it. Ellis said she would, but for him to fail. Ellis said that if he wanted to he could, but she still did not want to live.

The report from Prison Officer Griffin is important. It shows that Ruth was still adhering to her 'eye for an eye' stance and was still refusing to discuss who gave her the gun.

Although during her interview with George Rogers Ruth gave no indication that she was unhappy about the way John Bickford was handling her case, on every visit Bickford made to Holloway after her conviction Ruth accused him of sheltering the Findlaters and, in particular, Carole. In an effort to reassure her that he was doing all he could to get her a reprieve, Bickford wrote to the solicitors, Victor Mishcon & Co. of Brixton, seeking their help. Mr Mishcon passed the letter to his managing clerk, Mr Leon Simmons, who had handled her divorce from George Ellis and had met her frequently over the past three and a half years. On 30 June, Mr Simmons wrote a long letter to Major Lloyd-George detailing the background to her divorce and stressing that 'she was of a kind disposition and generous to a fault.' The letter was filed away, stamped 'Treat Officially' and ignored.

Despite increased pressure from her friends such as Jackie Dyer, her parents and her solicitor, Ruth still refused to seek a reprieve. In public her mother accepted Ruth's decision. Mr Godfrey Winn in the *Sunday Dispatch* on 3 July had reported that Ruth's mother, Mrs Neilson, had said:

'No new fact can help my daughter. A bird stripped of its fine feathers.' On 5 July, a week before the date fixed for her execution, she wrote to a friend, Mr Frank Neale. 'No dought [sic] you have heard that I do not want to live . . . You may find this very hard to believe, but that is what I want.'

Not all Ruth's letters from Holloway were so despondent. A few days after she shot David Blakely she wrote to Clive Gunnell who had left the Magdala pub with David on Easter Sunday night:

Dear Clive,

Thanks for your letter. No dought [sic] you have been shocked rather badly. Thanks for all the racing news, it is nice hearing all about Peter and the rest . . . Holloway is a jolly nice place better than Butling [sic] Holiday Camp you are always talking about peace and quite [sic].

Every one is jolly nice here it has surprised me . . . Sorry about the writing, the pen is definitely not my type at all. Has you know Mr Bickford is my lawyer I feel sure he will do his best, but I have no faulse (I have forgotten how to spell) idears about my position, so do not worry (friend) I shall be able to take it . . . Please excuse the writing paper, heading, but the printers could not get my own crest printed in time.

Well Clive I am in Court Hampstead Police Station on the 28th Thursday, so you will be reading more about things, so don't forget to order your copy right away.

Bye for now, Clive.
Thanks Once Again.
[signed] Ruth E.

There was another letter to a friend, Alex, who I have been unable to identify:

Dear Alex,

I am writing to you, again, because I hate the thought of you being without money. Perhaps you can get *another* £5 for this letter, like you got for the last one.

Yes, Alex, I still have a sense of humor.

Goodbye
[signed] Ruth Ellis

It's always nice to know, Alex, at a time like this, who's one's friends are.

On the morning of 11 July Ruth was told by Dr Charity Taylor, the Governor of Holloway, that there would be no reprieve. The full text of Major Lloyd-George's reasons for not recommending a reprieve are revealed in a memorandum signed by him now available at the Public Records Office. It is worth reprinting in full. By modern standards the Home Secretary does not emerge as a man troubled by the doubts of a humane conscience. But judged by the standards of the 1950s he was fulfilling his legal duty as Home Secretary.

I have given the most careful and anxious consideration to this case.

As I conceive my duty, it is to review all the circumstances of a capital case in order to see if there are such mitigating circumstances as would justify me in recommending interference with the due course of law. It is no part of the duty of a Home Secretary to give any weight to his own approval, or detestation, of the penalty prescribed by law; and least of all is it his duty to alter the law merely on the grounds that he thinks that a penalty which is appropriate for a man is inappropriate for a woman.

There may be circumstances in a capital case where special considerations apply to a woman which would not be applicable in the case of a man. A recent example is the case of Mrs Sarah Lloyd.* I can find no such special circumstances, however, in the present case. The crime was a premeditated one and was carried out with deliberation. The prisoner has expressed no remorse. I can find nothing to justify my taking a less serious view of this case than of other similar cases where the crime was of a callous and calculated nature.

I have been pressed from many quarters to exercise clemency in this case on the grounds of the prisoner's sex and of her yielding to jealousy which is alleged by some people to be stronger in the case of a woman than in the case of a man. But our law takes no special account of the so-called *crime passionel*, and I am not prepared to differentiate between the sexes on the grounds that one sex is more susceptible to jealousy than the other.

Cases may arise from time to time where a husband deserts a wife, or a wife deserts a husband, or where one spouse is deceived by the other spouse in the most provocative circumstances, and clemency may be appropriate

---

* On 6 May 1955 forty-year-old Mrs Sarah Lloyd had been sentenced to death at Leeds Assizes for the murder of her eighty-six-year-old neighbour, following a two-year domestic dispute between the two women. Mrs Lloyd was due to be executed on 7 July but was reprieved on 5 July.

in such a case. In the present instance, there is no such element; and the woman was as unfaithful to her lover as he was to her.

I have consulted the trial Judge and discussed all the details of the case with him. He told me that he was unable to suggest any mitigating circumstances, and although he naturally disowned any responsibility for the ultimate decision, he said that he himself could find no sufficient grounds for suggesting that clemency would be appropriate.

If a reprieve were granted in this case, I think that we should have seriously to consider whether capital punishment should be retained as a penalty.

The fact that many people have signed letters and petitions on behalf of the prisoner is a factor to which I have given due weight. I do not think that it is a conclusive factor.

After much anxious thought I have come to the conclusion that this is a case in which the law should be allowed to take its course.

The news that she would not be reprieved broke the mask of indifferent detachment that Ruth had maintained for so long. This indifference was based on a mixture of pride and religion. Ruth did believe that the law of God, to whom she had now returned in prison, demanded an eye for an eye. There was also the law of that part of the human jungle in which she had lived – the world of drunks, perverts, confidence tricksters and villains. 'Thou shalt not squeal' was their code.

United with this mixture of principles was Ruth's hope that she would be reprieved, a sentiment shared by her solicitor and which he used to comfort her. She could not really accept that any reasonable man like Major Lloyd-George would not see the justice of David's shooting. For a woman who had nothing but bad luck in her dealings with men, this was a most optimistic assumption.

Ruth's reaction to Dr Taylor's news was immensely human; she had hysterics and lay on her bed screaming 'I don't want to die.'

Fortunately for both Ruth and the two watching wardresses in the condemned cell, there were soon visitors, among them John Bickford and later George Rogers. John Bickford caught the first uncontrolled typhoon of fear and suspicion that now possessed her. In Ruth's eyes he had failed and deceived her. Before she died, she talked wildly about his 'treachery'. First there were the Findlaters, whom he had let escape, and now all his promises that she would be reprieved had failed. In a fury of resentment she told him that she wanted to see the solicitor who had acted for her in her divorce, Mr Victor Mishcon. Her reaction was understandable, but it was a complete misjudgement of John Bickford.

When George Rogers arrived (she had obviously forgiven him for his first visit fiasco) she was calmer but still deeply upset. Ruth asked him to get in touch with Victor Mishcon but did not discuss what she wanted to tell the solicitor. She agreed that Mr and Mrs Rogers should have Andy to stay with them for a holiday in the difficult days to come.

Despite Ruth's decision to fire him John Bickford refused to desert his client. After leaving Holloway he wrote to Victor Mishcon saying that Mrs Ellis wanted to see Mr Leon Simmons urgently as she had lost confidence in him.

He then wrote to the Home Office citing a statement from Mrs Dyer that Ruth and David Blakely had been drinking 'a great deal of spirits' for the last six months. The letter also included a statement from a Dr Symmonds who described himself as a 'specialist in alcoholism therapy'. Dr Symmonds said that 'Mrs Ellis was almost certainly an alcoholic and that many minds poisoned by alcohol could rationalise a murderous impulse which could result in a compulsive action when sober enough to attempt it.' The Home Office official who commented on these letters wrote: 'There seems to be nothing new here.' He was right.

Early on the morning of 12 July Messrs Mishcon and Simmons went to see John Bickford and asked him if there was anything they could ask Ruth Ellis that would even now help her. Bickford said that one aspect of the case was unanswered: who had given Ruth the gun. It was something that Ruth refused to allow him to mention at any Court hearing and had insisted that she had nothing to add to her statement to the police that she was given the Smith and Wesson in repayment for a loan. Mr Mishcon and Mr Simmons then went to Holloway and obtained the following statement from Ruth:

> I Ruth Ellis have been advised by Mr Victor Mishcon to tell the whole truth in regard to the circumstances leading up to the killing of David Blakely and it is only with the greatest reluctance that I have decided to tell how it was that I got the gun with which I shot Blakely. I did not do so before because I felt that I was needlessly getting someone into possible trouble.
>
> I had been drinking Pernod (I think that is how it is

spelt) in Desmond Cussen's flat and Desmond had been drinking too. This was about 8.30 p.m. We had been drinking for some time. I had been telling Desmond about Blakely's treatment of me. I was in a terribly depressed state. All I remember is that Desmond gave me a loaded gun. Desmond was jealous of Blakely as in fact Blakely was of Desmond. I would say that they hated each other. I was in such a dazed state that I cannot remember what was said. I rushed out as soon as he gave me the gun. He stayed in the flat. I rushed back after a second or two and said 'Will you drive me to Hampstead?' He did so and left me at the top of Tanza Road.

I had never seen that gun before. The only gun I had ever seen there was a small air pistol used as a game with a target.

After leaving Holloway, Ruth's new legal team took the statement to the Home Office and saw Mr Philip Allen, a senior official, who was in day-to-day charge of the case. His report of the meeting must have been based on the evidence of the wardress who monitored it. He wrote:

Mrs Ellis was under the clear impression at the beginning of the interview that all that was to be discussed was an alteration to her will and certain other legal documents. Mr Mishcon himself, however, asked Mrs Ellis whether she would not care to tell him about the gun with which Blakely had been shot. She repeatedly declined to say anything other than what she had already said in the proceedings. Mr Mishcon insisted that she should leave behind her a record of the truth, and Mr Simmons joined in the plea that she should do so in order that everyone, especially her own child, should know the truth. She at last said, 'You are the only person who has been able to persuade me to do this. I suppose the truth would have been found out anyway after I have gone. I will tell *you* what happened.' Mr Simmons said, 'Tell us what happened and we can discuss afterwards whether or not we have your permission to do anything with it.' She said, 'I didn't say anything about it up to now because it seemed traitorous – absolutely traitorous.' Mr Mishcon then took a statement from her, which is in Mr Mishcon's handwriting. He read it over to her and just before she signed it she said, 'There is one more thing. You had better know the whole truth', and she then added the words, which Mr Mishcon wrote into the statement, 'I rushed back after a second or two and said "Will you drive me to Hampstead?" He did so and left me at the top of Tanza Road.'

Mr Mishcon and Mr Simmons emphasised to Mrs Ellis that it was her duty to let the authorities know the truth and upon that basis obtained her consent to put the statement before the Home Secretary. She had not the slightest idea from first to last that this could make any difference to the question of reprieve and, in the discussion which then went on about the alteration to the will and legal documents, took it completely for granted that she would be executed tomorrow. She addressed no question to Mr Mishcon or Mr Simmons as to whether the statement would be taken to the Home Secretary today or would in fact only be put to him after she had been executed. Nor did she ask to see either of them again. She took it quite for granted that the Home Secretary's decision was final and that her statement was purely in order that the truth should be known before she died.

It is clear from this account that at this time Mr Allen had not seen the written report from Prison Officer Griffin and I assume he had been briefed over the phone by Dr Taylor, the Prison Governor. However, when the written report arrived it was to play an essential part in Home Office thinking later that day. Griffin's statement reads:

For your information I wish to state that I was present when Ellis was visited by her Solicitors Mr Simmons and Mr Mishcon.

Mr Mishcon was very persistent in asking Ellis about the gun, stating that it was only fair that the Home Secretary knew the true facts of the gun, he did not suppose it would help Ellis but the truth could be put on record. Ellis said that she didn't want to say anything that would get anyone else in trouble, the solicitor assured her it would not and if only she would tell him what he wanted to know, they would discuss it after and see if it would help her and after repeated attempts by Mr Mishcon Ellis, with very, very great reluctance said, alright I will tell you, but I can't in front of the Officer. After a little more persuasion Ellis said that she hadn't had the Gun for 3 years but was given it by Desmond Cousins [sic] on the night she shot Blakely (Easter Sunday). He loaded it, and oiled it before giving it to her. She says she was muddled through all the drink she had had and can't remember the conversation that passed when D. Cousins gave her the gun. She knows she was drinking Vurnat, a greenish liquid from 8.30 p.m., till 3 a.m., most days and she was dreadfully muddled, but clearly remembers rushing out of the room when given the gun. She came back a few moments later, and asked D. Cousins to drive her to Hamps [rest illegible] which he did without asking any questions. She had never seen the gun only an air pistol in the flat, Blakely was more jealous of Cousins than [missing word] of Blakeley [*sic*]. She still says she doesn't want to live, if she did, she [missing word] have pleaded Insanity at her trial. She said that she went to the flat with Desmond and it was her suggestion that she had the gun. The rest of [missing word] was to add a codicil to the will, making her Parents Executors and transfer?] the whole business to Mr Simmons.

The sting was in the tail. She confirmed that Desmond had given her the gun but it was 'at her suggestion'.

From the moment that she had been questioned at Hampstead police station after her arrest, the police had never believed Ruth's signed statement that the gun had been given to her three years previously as security for debt. All she would say, however, to further probing by Inspector Davies was that she had kept it hidden, wrapped in a towel. At the Magistrates' Court on 20 April, before she appeared in the dock, Inspector Davies had told her:

'We don't believe your story about the gun. Who gave it to you?' He mentioned a well-known West End criminal whose name was found in Ruth's diary. She replied 'No.'

Inspector Davies then said: 'Well, the gun was cleaned and oiled.' Ruth replied: 'Was it, I know nothing about it, I am sorry.'

When the gun was examined by police scientists, they found no trace of fluff or material on it. To be fair to the police, whenever they raised the subject of the gun with either Ruth or Desmond Cussen they got nowhere.

Shortly after Ruth had been committed to Holloway a Mrs Marie Harris, who gave Ruth French lessons at Cussen's flat at Goodwood Court, wrote to Scotland Yard saying she had seen 'a gun in a drawer at the flat'. The Yard contacted the Hampstead police and Inspector Davies and another officer searched the flat in Cussen's presence. He denied all knowledge of the gun, but the police found an air pistol and a starting pistol. The latter went off when Inspector Davies pulled the trigger.

On 25 June Jackie Dyer, prompted by George Rogers, wrote to the Home Secretary pleading for mercy for Ruth. In this letter Mrs Dyer said Ruth 'knew there was a gun at Cussen's flat'. In a Home Office memorandum of 4 July Mr Philip Allen notes Mrs Dyer's claim and reports that 'the police have made enquiries but they do not bear out that this is where Mrs Ellis obtained the gun.' He further commented: 'Although it would be more satisfactory if it could be established where the gun came from, and at what stage Mrs Ellis obtained it, it does not seem that this is really pertinent to the main question at issue, since there can be no doubt that Mrs Ellis armed herself with a gun some considerable time before she went out to Hampstead with the deliberate intention, on her own admission, of killing Blakely.' I find this statement baffling. If a crime has been committed it must be the duty of all authorities concerned to assemble all the facts and not give up when faced with difficulties.

Now that the truth about the gun was out even the ponderous machine that is the Home Office was forced to shift gear. The Permanent Under Secretary, Sir Frank Newsam, was at the Ascot races where, after a loudspeaker appeal, he took a phone call from Philip Allen asking him to return to London urgently.

During the day there had been other attempts to persuade the Home Secretary to change his mind. Some members of the London County Council appealed to Major Lloyd-George for a reprieve and Frank Owen, a noted journalist, and once Liberal MP for Hereford, sent the Home Secretary a telegram claiming that Ruth Ellis had had a miscarriage three days before she committed murder and that this perhaps had unhinged her mind. Mr Owen pointed out that if a child had been born, and Ruth had killed it, she would not have been hanged as the law ackncwledges that a woman may not be completely in control of herself after the birth of a baby. Mr Owen's motives were admirable, even if he had advanced the date of the miscarriage considerably. It occurred at least thirteen days before the shooting.

These appeals were as useless in helping to save Ruth Ellis as her last minute confession. Sir Frank Newsam got in touch with Scotland Yard and asked Mr Richard Jackson, the Assistant Commissioner for Crime, to see what could be done to find the man that Ruth named as the owner of the gun. The investigation of the case had not been a Scotland Yard affair, it had been left to Hampstead police. The senior officer was Superintendent Leonard Crawford but the day-to-day work had been done by Inspector Davies and Detective Constable Claiden. When Mr Jackson phoned from Scotland Yard to order the man who had investigated the crime to reopen the case, Superintendent Crawford was away on another murder investigation, and Inspector Davies was in bed with a heavy chill.

The only senior officer who knew of the case was

Detective Inspector Peter Gill, the officer who wrote down Ruth's original statement and who had also worked with Inspector Davies on the case. Gill and Claiden went to Goodwood Court to interview Desmond Cussen. They arrived around 9.30 p.m. but were too late. Cussen had left at about 9.15 p.m. carrying a suitcase, telling the porter that he was going to the country. He told the porter that he wanted to get away to avoid reporters and asked him to check if the street was clear. The porter did so and Cussen drove off in his black Ford Zodiac. He returned to Goodwood Court three weeks later. The two policemen waited in the lobby until about 10.00 p.m. and then left. They went to the Red Lion pub in Whitehall where they were found by Inspector Davies. The three of them agreed that there was nothing more they could do; London is a large place to find someone who is not at home. Inspector Davies then phoned the Home Office to report failure.

At the Home Office Philip Allen commented that he had interviewed the prison officer who had been present when Ruth made her statement to Victor Mishcon and that the fact that Ellis had asked Cussen for the gun was important. Sir Frank Newsam said: 'The uncorroborated evidence by the prisoner does not add anything material to the information before the Secretary of State when he decided not to interfere. The discrepancy between the officer's report and Mr Mishcon's statement is interesting and illuminating.'

Ruth Ellis was doomed.

She herself seems to have recognised this long before the search was abandoned, for she gave neither her parents nor Mrs Dyer, who visited her that day, any sign that she expected her last minute confession to gain her a reprieve.

It was Ruth who comforted her mother in two heart-wrenching good-bye meetings between them. She asked her mother to go to Penn after the execution and put red and white carnations on David's grave. David had sent her this colour combination in the carnations which accompanied his 'I love you' note after their last major row.

To Mrs Dyer she said: 'Have you heard the big news? I'm not going to be reprieved. Don't worry, it's like having a tooth out and they'll give me a glass of brandy beforehand.' Her calm was now as marked as the iron indifference that had shielded her in the weeks following David's shooting.

Nobody then or later had a complete answer as to why Ruth Ellis murdered David Blakely in such a detached and remorseless fashion, encapsulated in her evidence to Mr Melford Stevenson at the Old Bailey:

Mr Stevenson: And we have had the evidence about your taking a revolver up to Hampstead and shooting him. Is that right?

A. Quite correct.

Q Why did you do it?

A. I do not really know, quite seriously. I was just very upset.

Mr Justice Havers: 'I do not really know why I shot him.' Is that right?

A. Yes.

Mr Justice Havers: 'I was very upset'?

A. Yes.

Mr Stevenson: When you say you had a peculiar idea that you wanted to kill him, were you able to control it?

A. No.

Q And then you went up in fact and shot him? Is that
   right?
A. Yes.


I believe that Ruth Ellis shot her lover because she was temporarily insane with jealousy and humiliation, and her sense
of responsibility was destroyed by alcohol. She had, as she
told Inspector Davies, 'a few drinks before I shot him'. In
those last few months she was an alcoholic, and even a 'few'
drinks would be sufficient to cement the illusions of a real
drunkard that whatever he or she does is unquestionably
right. To her it was right that David should die; he had
destroyed her and humiliated her. It was an intolerable position which, to someone as emotionally immature as Ruth
Ellis, could only be resolved in violence.

The fires of her jealous insecurity had been continuously
stoked during the last week before the murder. Whatever
moments of tenderness there had been, the visit to the cinema and the gift of the photograph, were obliterated by the
realization that David would never marry her. She was sure
that he was being unfaithful to her with a girl thrown at
him by her enemy Mrs Findlater. All the illusions about
'being somebody' had disappeared.

In the past she had always got David back by one means
or another. Now when she sat smoking and brooding all
night during that Easter weekend she realized that she did
not want him back any more. The most important outward
sign of this decision was the removal of his photograph
from the room at No. 44 Egerton Gardens. It was that
room, as much as anything, that made Ruth realize what
David had done to 'ruin' her; not so much materially,
although that was bad enough, but in the estimation of the

rest of her world. Materially he had, she reasoned, brought her down from the manageress of a first class drinking club to an out-of-work failed trainee model. The woman who once had pounds to waste had sixpence in copper in her bag when she was arrested and nothing in the bank. The poverty that she had always feared was here. Once, she wrote later, she had been 'good company and fun to be with. He had turned me into a surly and miserable woman. I was growing to loathe him, he was conceited and said all women loved him. He was so much in love with himself.'

There was no love to restrain her, for love in the sense of mutual consideration, understanding and sacrifice had never existed between them. To David love had meant lust. To Ruth it was a combination of temporarily satisfied pride and the promise of ambitions to be achieved without real sacrifice; the realization of the unchartable illusions of Ruth Ellis.

Thousands of women feel similar emotions about men who have used and deserted them but, in Britain, mercifully few move beyond the urge to hurt the man. Ruth Ellis was no conventional woman. She never thought of her children before she shot David; she had an immense concentrated determination, shown in her unflagging jealous searches for both her husband and her lover. Those who slept with her report that her attitude during the sexual act was dominant and unyielding. 'She had,' said one customer 'a very masculine approach to sex.'

Unlike most women, her life after the birth of her illegitimate son had conditioned her to the easy talk of violence. Her world was the land of 'shooters', where guns are bought and sold like tea. This familiarity with gangster talk and behaviour was buttressed by her reading of pulp stories of sex that ended in blood and death.

Tragically for her when the frenzy of her destroyed pride and ambitions erupted, there was a Smith and Wesson to hand.

Ruth was dominated in the getting of the gun and in the use of it by that unhappy gift of poor luck that intruded in moments of importance during her life. With good luck she might never have fatally wounded David, for when the gun was test-fired after the murder the cylinder catch broke 'due to a long-standing fault in the mechanism'.

On 12 July, the day before her execution, Ruth had a set of dejected visitors who found her composed and resigned. Outside Holloway the atmosphere was British. The inevitable crowd of zombies with their lolly-licking children had been there most of the day watching the last comings and goings of the relatives and other visitors to the woman who was to be hanged in their name. Portable radios among them provided a commentary on the Test Match, and, at intervals, jazz.

The men were shirt-sleeved in the wonderful July sun, the women wore cheerful cottons. At teatime, Mr Albert Pierrepoint, the hangman, arrived by taxi. Some of the crowd stayed outside the prison gates after dark.

They chanted 'Evans, Bentley, Ellis', and hammered on the great wooden double doors of the prison until the police moved them to the other side of the road. To increase the tension, someone called the fire brigade to a false alarm near the prison.

Inside, Ruth Ellis was calmly writing her last letters; she refused to see her brother Granville who had called, hoping to visit his sister, for the third time that day. She wrote to George Rogers giving him authority to have Andria, who was staying with one of her sisters, for a holiday. Her letter ended: 'I am quite well – my family have been wonderful. Once again I thank you and your wife.

Good-bye, Ruth Ellis.'

She wrote to one of her friends, Frank Neale, thanking him for his last letter 'or should I say epistle, I enjoyed reading it . . . but never mind friend we will all meet again, not to worry.'

She was willing to meet her God, the God of vengeance and retribution. Ruth Ellis was up early on the last morning of her life at about half-past six. The bravery of her final hours was almost inhuman, with no tears, no scaffold regret; instead she wrote more letters of farewell. To Mr Simmons, Victor Mishcon's managing clerk, she said:

> Just to let you know I am still feeling alright. The time is 7 o'clock a.m. – everyone is simply wonderful in (STAFF) Holloway. This is just for you to console my family with the thought that I did not change my way of thinking at the last moment.
>
> Or break my promise to David's mother.
>
> Well Mr Simmons, I have told you the truth and that's all I can do.
>
> Thanks once again.
>
> Goodbye
> Ruth Ellis.

In another letter to Mr Simmons: 'I am now content and satisfied that my affairs will be dealt with satisfactorily. I also ask you to make known the true story regarding Mrs Findlater and her plan to break up David and I – she should be content now her plan ended so tragically. Would you please ask my mother to go to David's grave and place flowers, pink and white carnations (ask her to do it for me).'

Outside the prison in the clear sunlight about one thousand men, women and children were jostling and waiting.

Ruth's parents were not among the crowd. They had been up all night in Hemel Hempstead drinking the inevitable incessant cups of tea, still hoping that the Home Secretary would be merciful and give the reprieve which Mrs Neilson had begged for in her letter.

In Holloway Ruth knelt as the Catholic priest gave as much comfort as he could; at her request a crucifix was fastened to the wall of the execution shed next to the condemned cell so that she might see it momentarily before she died.

In Blackpool the Chamber of Horrors in the waxworks on the Golden Mile was being reorganized to exhibit an effigy of Ruth in a black evening gown.

In Harrow her son Andria was talking to Mrs George Rogers and complaining that he had come to stay in a funny house where they had no newspapers or radio. He believed that his mother had gone to Italy to model swimwear and was not worried that she had not written.

Outside the prison the crowd strained for the notice of execution to be affixed to the gates, and a street musician played on his violin 'Be Thou with me when I die'. In Hemel Hempstead her father started to play a lament on his 'cello and her mother, unable to cry, went upstairs to pray.

In Middlesex, the headmaster of a boys' school walked through the playground and saw four of his pupils, all under the age of eleven, standing still; one of them had a watch in his hand. He was saying: 'Only four more minutes and she is going to swing. One, two, three, four, she has had it boys.'

After she knelt in prayer before the cross on the cell wall they gave Ruth Ellis the promised glass of brandy. Albert Pierrepoint strapped Ruth's hands behind her back and they walked the few steps from the condemned cell to the adjoining execution shed.

Until the last moment of her life drama did not desert her as this memorandum from Dr Charity Taylor shows:

With reference to the execution of the above-named woman, I beg to report that at 8.55 a.m. approx to-day I received a telephone call from a Miss or Mrs Holmes who stated that she was private secretary to Major Lloyd-George. She said that a stay of execution was on its way in the case of Ruth Ellis. I said I must check this and that I would telephone back to the Home Office to confirm the message. I telephoned the Home Office telephone number, but could not trace a Miss or Mrs Holmes, or that any such message had been given out. I tried to telephone Mr Guppy, Private Secretary, but he was not at the Home Office, and had just left his home. Mrs Forbes, the other Private Secretary, was not available. This caused some delay, and in view of the unsatisfactory source of the message, and after consultation with the Under-Sheriff, Mr Gedge, it was decided to carry on with the execution. This was done, and the execution took place at 9.1 a.m. instead of 9 a.m. as arranged.

At 9.5 a.m. Mrs Forbes telephoned stating that she had not telephoned the Governor, but that the Governor had telephoned her.

Mr Guppy spoke to me afterwards regarding the incident.

Later, the public executioner said that: 'she wobbled a bit, but otherwise she gave him no trouble. She was as good as bloody gold, she was.'

Most of the circumstances about the life and death of Ruth Ellis have now been revealed. Only one major question remains unanswered. Why did Desmond Cussen agree to give her the gun? One reason could have been that he was so jealous of David Blakely that he saw David's death as the only solution. I do not believe this. In the three months between Ruth Ellis's arrest and execution I spent hours with Cussen getting much of the background information about his relationship with Ruth which John Bickford used to prepare his defence.

I did not find Desmond Cussen a likeable man but what did emerge was a very cool and determined operator. But it was also clear that he was besotted with Ruth, despite the fact that she had always treated him like a poodle. He paid the rent at Egerton Gardens for her but David got all the sexual favours. She had no money, Desmond paid Andy's boarding school fees. She had no car, Desmond drove her wherever she wanted to go. If she had told him to jump off Beachy Head I'm certain he would have thought very seriously about it.

In 1962 when I decided to write the Ruth Ellis story I phoned Desmond who was still at Goodwood Court and we met for a drink. I asked him whether he was still upset about Ruth's death. He said, 'It's no good keeping going over and over things. What's done's done, it can't be changed now.' I said, 'I'm going to write a book about it, and I'm pretty sure you gave her the gun, what do you want to say about it?' He was completely unfazed by the question. 'You know as well as I do that I told Inspector Davies I knew nothing about a gun and that's that.'

We had a few more drinks and dropped the subject. Then as we were about to leave the pub Desmond said, 'If I were writing your book I'd say the man who gave her the gun never thought she'd use it. You see he must have known that if she shot Blakely she would either be hanged or go to prison for a long while. So I think you should say that Ruth told him that she knew someone who would shoot David for her but she had to get a gun for him.' He added, 'And if you say this is what I told you I'll call you a liar and ask my lawyer to deal with you.' He refused to talk any more and left the pub without me.

When I first wrote the book I suggested that an unnamed man had given Ruth the gun believing that she in turn would pass it on to a hit man.

How far does Desmond's suggestion square with the known facts? In her statement on the eve of her execution Ruth said that after Desmond gave her the gun he stayed in the flat and it was only after she came back that she told him to drive her to Tanza Road, Hampstead. In her account of the death cell confession Prison Officer Griffin said that Desmond drove her to Hampstead without asking any questions. The officer also said that Ruth had asked Desmond for the gun. In short, once again, Desmond was doing what he was told.

When they set off for Tanza Road did Desmond really believe Ruth was going to deliver the gun to a hit man? Your guess is as good as mine.

# Epilogue

The controversy that surrounded the hanging of Ruth Ellis has never ceased. It has spawned seventeen books, two TV documentaries and a film *Dance with a Stranger*. The flood started a few days after her death and, not surprisingly, Major Gwilym Lloyd-George was in the firing line. The *Spectator* magazine published two articles savaging his handling of the case. Clearly stung, the Home Secretary wrote to the Lord Chancellor, Lord Kilmuir:

> . . . My first inclination was to treat the articles with the contempt they deserve. On further reflection I am not altogether sure that this would be right. It is one thing to say that the Home Secretary is incompetent: no one can complain about that; but it is another to say that he is incompetent because he spends his time in the smoking room and neglects his official duties, and acts under pressure from his advisers. You know how much anxious care has always been devoted to the consideration of capital cases. I have tried to the best of my ability and conscience to continue that tradition . . . I should be very grateful if you would consider the articles and let me know what you think would be the right course for me to take.

Three days later he got a sensible reply:

. . . I do not think that you should take action for the following reasons.

1. Broadly, we who go into the arena of public life must get dirt and worse (I have had a fair share myself on the same ground).

2. A cross-examination on how a Home Secretary comes to his decisions would be used as an abolitionist field-day, and would rouse controversy to fever point.

3. Although I think that any Minister who does not go regularly to the smoking room is not doing his job properly, and have always acted on this view, I do not think that it would be a good thing for the dignity of government that this should be canvassed.

4. Again, I do not see how the suggestion of acting under pressure of officials could be canvassed in Court without either going into advice given to Ministers or putting such a stop by a use of Crown Privilege as would make the fairness of the trial suspect.

5. I should not think the circulation of the *Spectator* is more than 25,000 or that its mouthings will be remembered for even the traditional nine days.

6. The letters in the second number show an impressive amount of support for you and disgust with the first article.

7. No one could possibly think the worse of you for not taking action against so miserable an attack.

As I have indicated, the very hysteria with which this sort of stuff is produced makes it more ephemeral than most, and as a lawyer, an ex-Home Secretary and an old friend I advise you to let it die in its own smell.

Major Lloyd-George, later Viscount Tenby, did little to enhance his reputation in a speech he made in York a few months later. He told his audience that sometimes he thought it would be a good thing if the Russians and the Chinese played cricket, 'only heaven help the fellow who ran the Captain out'.

The next attack on the verdict came from Mr Peter Grisewood, a journalist who interviewed most of the witnesses in the case, some of whom had not been called at the Old Bailey, and of course John Bickford. He sold the results to the *People* newspaper, who used it as the basis for a series of articles written by Mr Duncan Webb, a very respectable crime reporter. After the series had finished Grisewood took a lengthy memorandum to the Home Office which was analysed in detail in the following Home Office Minute dated 28 February 1956:

1. Mr Peter Grisewood left the memorandum within with Lord Mancroft. It embodies the fruits of his researches into the case of Ruth Ellis. Mr Grisewood's conclusions may be summarised as follows:-

   That Desmond Cussen gave Ruth Ellis the gun with which she shot Blakely, and drove her in his car near to the place where she later did the shooting; that Cussen played on Ruth Ellis' jealousy and made her drunk, and incited her to get rid of his rival; that Cussen arranged for Ruth Ellis to be represented by a Mr Bickford, with whom he was on friendly terms, and that the defence was so managed that Cussen's part in the proceedings was concealed; that Cussen committed perjury at the trial in saying that he could not remember the events of the day of the crime; and that the police did not investigate the crime thoroughly.

2. The fact that Ruth Ellis alleged that she obtained the gun from Cussen, and that he drove her to the scene of the

crime was known to the Secretary of State, since she signed a statement to this effect in prison (./14). On the assumption that the allegation was true, and bearing in mind Ruth Ellis' own statement – not included in the signed statement – that it was at her suggestion that Cussen gave her the gun, there was nothing in this that could have justified a reprieve. The statement that Cussen incited Ruth Ellis to commit the crime is new, but even if true it could not have affected the question of a reprieve, since it would not have substantially lessened her guilt. She was, after all, an adult of normal intelligence.

3. The conduct of the defence was entirely a matter for Ruth Ellis, and it was open to her to change her advisers at any time. If she was advised that she had a better chance if Cussen's part was not revealed, she may well have concluded that this was sound advice. If she had changed her advisers and brought out the full story about Cussen – assuming it to be true—it might have led to Cussen being indicted also, but it could not have helped her materially.

4. Cussen may have committed perjury at the trial, if the statement made by Ruth Ellis in prison is true, but he did not, as Mr Grisewood alleges, say that he could not remember the events of the day on which the crime was committed. He gave no answer of this sort at all.

5. A more difficult question is whether a prosecution would not lie against Cussen for being an accessory before the fact to the murder. In considering this it must be borne in mind that the principal witness, Ruth Ellis, can no longer testify, and that it would be open to Cussen to give any version he chose of the events on the day in question. There might be evidence from Ruth Ellis'

son* that Cussen offered to give her his gun, and it might be possible to prove that Cussen and Ruth Ellis were together in Cussen's flat in the evening, and then drove together to the neighbourhood of the crime. If it is thought desirable to pursue the matter further the papers might be brought to the notice of the Director of Public Prosecutions, who could advise what lines a further police investigation might take; but on public grounds there is a good deal to be said for not re-opening the case. We must, however, bear in mind the possibility that the contents of Mr Grisewood's memorandum may be made public at any time, and that the Secretary of State might then be questioned on this point. The similar revelations in *The People* have not, however, yet led to any questions about the case.

Mr Grisewood's memorandum and the Home Office comments were forwarded to the Director of Public Prosecutions who took no action. Perhaps this decision was based on the Home Office's official judgement that 'on public grounds there is a good deal to be said for not reopening the case' – whatever that cryptic phrase might mean. It is interesting that the box relating to the DPP documents in the case of Ruth Ellis is still (at the time of writing) unavailable at the Public Records Office.

The charge by Mr Grisewood that Bickford was a friend of Desmond Cussen is rubbish. The statement that Cussen had arranged for Bickford to represent Mrs Ellis is equally untrue. John Bickford had been briefed by a woman friend

---

* Neither the police nor any newspaper had interviewed Andy at the time. The thought of involving a ten year old in giving evidence against his mother easily carried the day. Times have changed.

of Ruth's but all costs of her defence were paid for by *The Woman's Sunday Mirror*.

In a Thames Television documentary screened in 1977, Bickford gave his explanation of his conduct in the defence of Ruth Ellis. He vehemently denied that he had ever been bribed by Desmond Cussen to hide his part in the crime. But he did admit that he had known all along that Cussen had given Ruth the gun and driven her to Hampstead on the night of the murder. Bickford said that Ruth Ellis had told him the truth about the origin of the gun at his first visit to her at Holloway. When he faced Cussen with the admission Cussen agreed it was true.

Interviewed on television Bickford said he had not told the police about Cussen's involvement because Ruth had forbidden him to do so and legal etiquette meant he must obey his client's instructions. Asked why, when Ruth had fired him and sent for Victor Mishcon, he had not told Mishcon the truth, Bickford said that although he was sacked, Ruth had not freed him from his obligation to keep quiet about Cussen's involvement. He said: 'I went as far as I could by telling Victor Mishcon to press Ruth to tell the truth about the gun. Perhaps I made a mistake. I'm sorry and in that case I should apologise to Ruth Ellis.'

John Bickford 'confessed' that Ruth had told him Cussen had given her the gun and driven her to Hampstead. Was he telling the truth? He made this revelation in the documentary when Home Office papers on the case were unavailable. When those papers were available they recorded Philip Allen's account of his meeting with Victor Mishcon and Leon Simmons after they had seen Mrs Ellis that morning (12 July) at Holloway.

Victor Mishcon and Leon Simmons repeatedly urged Ruth to tell the truth about who gave her the gun. Finally, she said to Mr Simmons: 'I will tell you what happened. You are the only person who has been able to persuade me to do this.' She later added: 'I didn't say anything up to now because it seemed traitorous – absolutely traitorous.' This evidence must raise doubts about John Bickford's 'confession'.

A more cynical explanation is that when Thames planned their film, John Bickford was very short of money. He realised that unless he could provide some sensational facts about the case it might be difficult to sell the documentary. Hence his visit to Scotland Yard some twenty years after Ruth's death to provide new facts about the case.

Some time before the screening of the television documentary Bickford had gone to Scotland Yard and made a statement admitting that he had known from the start that Cussen had given Ruth the gun and that she had admitted it. He made this confession, he said, because his silence in the matter had haunted him for years. The authorities took no action.

There is a third possible explanation for Bickford's action. At the time the film was made, John Bickford was a very heavy drinker, a drunk. It could be that he had always suspected Desmond Cussen had given Ruth the gun and that heavy drinking over many years had transformed this theory into fact in his mind. Your guess is as good as mine.

Would it have saved Ruth from the gallows if Bickford had gone to the police before her trial? The Home Office memo is clear that 'it might have led to Cussen being indicted also, but it could not have helped her materially.'

Cussen's reaction to Bickford's part in the TV programme was predictable. A Thames TV reporter went to

Perth in Australia where Cussen had opened a flower shop. He showed Cussen Bickford's statements in the programme and Cussen said: 'I did not give Ruth the gun. I did not drive her to Hampstead.'

One important reason that Bickford had kept quiet, apart from Ruth's insistence that Cussen should not be involved in the case, was that Bickford knew that Ruth was doomed if Cussen was charged either as a principal or as an accessory. The law then did not take a lenient view of conspiracy in a capital case.

In November 1999, the BBC transmitted a drama documentary on the Ruth Ellis case entitled *A Life for a Life*. It was a well-researched programme containing some information not available at Ruth's trial. Ruth's sister, Mrs Muriel Jakubait revealed that both she and her sister had been raped and abused when young children by their father, a crime accepted by their mother. Dr Gillian Mezey, a consultant forensic psychiatrist, commenting on this revelation judged that this childhood ordeal, plus all Ruth's unhappy and sometimes violent relationships with men, could have had an important bearing on her state of mind when she shot Blakely.

Today, of course, this evidence would have had great importance in any plea by Ruth of diminished responsibility or provocation. Unfortunately, even if such evidence had been produced at her trial, it would not, given the law as it stood in 1955, have altered the verdict. It might have provided a recommendation to mercy from the jury but I doubt it.

The main thrust of the programme was that the Home Office did not give the police enough time to find Cussen once Victor Mishcon had taken Ruth's confession to Whitehall. There should have been a stay of execution until Cussen was found and questioned. No stay was granted. Philip Allen, the Assistant Permanent Under Secretary, was reinforced in this decision to let the execution proceed because the prison officer's evidence was clear – Ruth had asked Cussen for the gun. His boss, Sir Frank Newsam, thought that the uncorroborated evidence of the prisoner added nothing new and that the discrepancy between the prison officer's statement and Ruth's was interesting and illuminating.

In the BBC TV programme Philip Allen admitted 'perhaps we were wrong.' This is, of course, based on hindsight.

The programme also attacked the Home Secretary's opinion that 'if a reprieve were granted in this case I think we should have to seriously consider whether capital punishment should be retained as a "penalty".' Kirsty Wark, who fronted the programme, asked Philip Allen whether this was a political stance by the Home Secretary and one that had prevented him from granting a reprieve. Philip Allen replied without hesitation: 'No, I don't think so.'

I agree; anyone who reads Major Lloyd-George's statement on the reasons why he had refused a reprieve (see pp. 177-8) can see that this observation is only one part of a detailed memorandum. It was certainly not the prime reason for his refusal to reprieve. It should be remembered that a week or so before Ruth's execution, Major Lloyd-George had reprieved Mrs Lloyd, a convicted murderer. Kirsty Wark did not mention this. She did press on, questioning Philip Allen on whether Ruth would have hanged if there had been a stay of execution until the police found Cussen. Allen replied: 'If it had involved a prolonged delay and a lot of further enquiries I think probably not.'

The answer must be speculation. We now know that Cussen returned to his flat at Goodwood Court about three

THE LAST WOMAN TO BE HANGED

weeks after the execution. If there had been a stay of execution for three weeks would that have been a 'prolonged delay'? If Cussen had confessed his part in the murder would it have taken long to try him and would Ruth then have given evidence against him? Her last minute confession, plus Home Office documents now available, show that she only confessed about the gun under great pressure from Mr Mishcon and she did not believe that it would have saved her life.

Even if we assume she would have given evidence against Cussen, either as a principal or an accessory, I doubt whether it would have altered the fact that she had been found guilty of a cruel and premeditated crime. Maybe the delay involved in bringing Cussen to trial would have resulted in a stay of execution, but given the reaction to her case by the majority of the public at the time, I doubt it.

Perhaps the most likely result of any police enquiries once Cussen had returned home would have been what he had maintained from the outset until his death in Australia: 'I never gave Ruth the gun.' If he had stuck to this in court would the jury have believed him or Ruth's scaffold confession? I question whether the prosecution could have made their charge stick 'beyond reasonable doubt'.

There are still some unrevealed clues in the Ruth Ellis story. It would be very interesting to read what prison officers recorded about what was said by Ruth to her parents and friends when they visited her in Holloway. Unfortunately, these records are missing from the papers at the Public Record Office. They were stolen from a storage cupboard at Holloway in January 1964. In December 1967 a prisoner at Pentonville Prison told the authorities that the missing papers might be in the hands of a man who ran a club in

Hammersmith, West London, who planned to sell them in the USA. They are still missing.

Ruth's death did not exorcise the mantra of tragedy that enveloped the principal players in the drama of her life. In 1958 her former husband George Ellis committed suicide, hanging himself by his pyjama cord in a Jersey Hotel. Ruth's mother, Bertha, attempted to end her life but failed. For the rest of her life she refused to discuss the case or have it discussed in her presence. Ruth's daughter, Georgina, was brought up by caring foster parents and grew up to become a model and lead a colourful life as the some-time lover of the footballer, George Best, and Richard Harris, the reputed hell-raiser and actor.

In 1971 Ruth's body was removed from Holloway to facilitate the rebuilding of the prison. She was re-interred in a churchyard in Amersham, Bucks. The headstone records her family name of Hornby; her father had changed it to Neilson for his stage work as a musician. One day Ruth's son Andria, who never recovered emotionally from his early experiences and the public attention forced on him by his mother's death, went to the churchyard and smashed the headstone. It was subsequently restored. In 1982, Andria, then 36, died from an overdose. He had led such a solitary life that it was three weeks before his body was found.

Carole Findlater, who Ruth had blamed, together with her husband Ant, as the real cause of her problems, also died from a drug overdose.

Perhaps the saddest figure in this almost Greek tragedy was John Bickford. Not long after Ruth's death he left Cardew, Smith & Ross, the London firm of solicitors in which he had been a partner. Shattered by his failure to obtain a reprieve for his client he began to drink heavily. An attempt to practice on his own as a solicitor ended in a severe reprimand from the Law Society for his questionable handling of his clients' affairs. He went to live in Malta where he opened and shut an unsuccessful bar. Despite warnings from friends he conducted a vigorous campaign against what he saw as local government abuses and was expelled from the country and returned to England in 1973. Flat broke he got a job with the Automobile Association as a part-time lawyer. His drink problem was now lethal and shortly after the screening of the Thames Television documentary on Ruth Ellis in 1977, he died.

On a happier note, in 1978 Victor Mishcon became a Life Peer, Baron Mishcon of Lambeth, and the lawyer whose firm handled Princess Diana's divorce from Prince Charles. In 1976 Philip Allen was created a Life Peer, Baron Allen of Abbeydale. Among his other achievements he was Chairman of the Gaming Board of Great Britain and Mencap.

And there is no dispute that the death of Ruth Ellis swelled the force of public opinion that finally ended the death penalty.